102 ENGLISH
THINGS TO DO

ALEX QUICK

First published in 2012 by Old Street Publishing Ltd,
Trebinshun House, Brecon LD3 7PX
www.oldstreetpublishing.co.uk

ISBN 978 1 908699 00 8

10 9 8 7 6 5 4 3 2 1

A CIP catalogue record for this title is available from the British Library.

Printed and bound in Great Britain by CPI Group (UK) Ltd, Croydon, CR0 4YY

102 ENGLISH
THINGS TO DO

CONTENTS

CONTENTS

Introduction

English attitudes

English manners

20.   Pretend it didn't happen

English behaviour

21.   Cultivate eccentricity
22.   Dress like a chap or chappess
23.   Dress entirely in dead people's clothing
24.   Bare your flesh
25.   Go to sleep in a deck chair on the beach
       wearing lots of clothes, because of the cold
26.   Show visitors your airing cupboard
27.   Buy a gnome
28.   Sit in a cottage garden full of hollyhocks
29.   Retreat to your shed

English entertainments

30.   Visit the V&A
31.   Go to the Notting Hill Carnival
32.   Visit Glyndebourne
33.   Go to the Proms
35.   Watch *Coronation Street*
36.   Watch an Ealing Comedy
37.   See a Punch and Judy show
38.   Listen to the Shipping Forecast
39.   Go to a finger-in-the-ear folk performance
       and join in the chorus

English crimes

39.   Riot
40.   Act like a hooligan
41.   Go on a country house murder weekend

42. Succumb to the English vice/English disease
43. Obsess over Lord Lucan
44. Have sex at 15
45. Go on a Jack the Ripper tour
46. Visit Baker Street

English language

47. Be nice
48. Be parliamentary
49. Read *Private Eye*
50. Write a clerihew
51. Browse in Charing Cross Road
52. Fail to learn any other languages
53. Speak in Cockney rhyming slang
54. Recite 'Invictus'
55. Read a book by PG Wodehouse
56. Read a book by Barbara Cartland

English activities

57. Sing 'Jerusalem'
58. Send a naughty postcard
59. Build something with Meccano
60. Walk an English Setter
61. Drive a Mini
62. Ride a Routemaster
63. Go to a jumble sale
64. Go punting at Oxford or Cambridge
65. Bike to Holy Communion through the mists of an autumn morning
66. Go change-ringing

67. Beat the Bounds
68. Celebrate Guy Fawkes' Night
69. Support a fringe party
70. Attend a Swan Upping
71. Do the Furry Dance

English sports

72. Play Poohsticks
73. Play croquet
74. Play cricket
75. Play conkers
76. Go on a fun run
77. Go extreme ironing
78. Eat nettles
79. Go toe-wrestling
80. Go cheese-rolling
81. Go bottle-kicking
82. Run in a pancake race
83. Go gurning

English places

84. Visit Parliament
85. Go to Greenwich
86. Visit an AONB
87. Visit Anne Hathaway's cottage
88. Visit Hadrian's Wall
89. Visit the Cerne Abbas Giant and the Uffington White Horse
90. Visit Stonehenge
91. Climb Scafell Pike

English food and drink

92.   Have a nice cup of tea
93.   Have a nice tea
94.   Eat a Full English
95.   Eat fish and chips
96.   Eat pie, mash and liquor
97.   Eat a real Cornish pasty made in Cornwall
98.   Stop at a St George's Cross motorway burger stand
99.   Savour an English apple
100.   Drink traditional cider
101.   Visit a beer festival
102.   Boil vegetables for as long as it takes for them to lose any flavour, texture or colour

INTRODUCTION

England is a confusing place. For a start, the name. Some say Britain when they mean England. Some say England when they mean Britain. Some, wishing to be flattering or patriotic, say Great Britain; others say the United Kingdom (despite the fact that it is ruled by a queen); others say the British Isles, though they may risk offending the Republic of Ireland.

Politically, the situation is no better. The parliament at Westminster in London is not the English parliament, it's the United Kingdom parliament. The other countries of the United Kingdom – Scotland, Wales and Northern Ireland – have their own devolved parliaments, but only England, the dominant partner, doesn't actually have its own seat of government.

The English are sometimes curiously self-effacing, as if they wish they weren't really there.

And yet this diffident country managed some remarkable things. It exported its language all over the world, penned a globally-renowned literature, kick-started the Enlightenment, and invented most of the world's sports. This would surely have been impossible without some sense of collective identity.

And it's true that English people, whether from Yorkshire or Norfolk, Bradford or Virginia Water, do still have a lot in common. Most of them buy their round at the pub, talk about the weather, understand the same ironic humour, say 'please' and 'thank you', treat tea like a religion, form an orderly queue, read the same newspapers, watch the same TV programmes (trashy ones), and feel something quivering in their chests when they hear the opening bars of 'Jerusalem'. England and the English have a discrete identity at least as real as Spain and the Spanish or Tibet and the Tibetans.

Perhaps the difficult thing to do is get the required distance. Englishness is only perceptible if considered from above, as if from a visiting spaceship. Then it all comes into focus and makes sense. From the right distance, there are English things to do, English things to eat, English things to think and feel... even English crimes to commit.

So that's the approach taken in this book. I want you to imagine yourself hovering somewhere above Fenny Drayton, Leicestershire, the geographical centre-point of England.

Now descend, slowly...

ENGLISH ATTITUDES

1.

IGNORE ENGLAND'S ACHIEVEMENTS

In the period from the sixteenth to the twentieth century, England managed to assemble the largest empire the world has ever seen. Starting with Scotland, Wales and Ireland, she went on to grab India, America, various bits of Africa, Canada, Australia, New Zealand and sundry other places, adding up to 13,010,000 square miles, or around a quarter of the globe.

Most English people now regard this spasm of acquisitiveness with a mixture of rueful pride and embarrassment, like a sporting injury.

The truth is that the English don't like to be reminded of England's achievements. The industrial revolution started in England and the World Wide Web was invented by an Englishman: the two greatest revolutions of the last three centuries, and they were essentially English. But English people will never be found crowing about them (except perhaps at Olympic opening ceremonies, and leavened with a hefty dose of irony: see No. 6 'Be Ironic'). They suspect, rightly, that they will be branded by other English people as being rather nationalistic – even racist – if they do.

Try mentioning to an English person that the Nobel Prize for Literature has been won twice in the last decade by an English writer, and they will almost certainly not be able to produce the required names (Harold Pinter and Doris Lessing).

Imagine if these prizes had been won by the Scots!

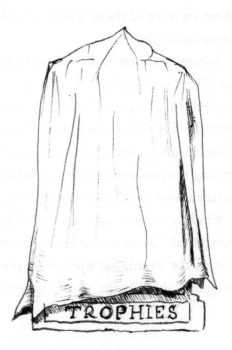

2.

DWELL ON ENGLAND'S FAILURES

There is a perfect antidote to English shame at England's achievements: England's failures. Fortunately there are a lot of these, and they make excellent conversational subjects.

For example, the English consider English food to be inedible. Even the French are not as disparaging about English cuisine as the English themselves. This is despite the fact that in the last couple of decades English food has undergone something of a renaissance. Mentioning this, however, is taboo. English culinary incompetence is too much of a treasure to give up.

English trains are always late, crowded and overpriced. Of course, they are worse in 95% of the rest of the world, but the rest of the world does not complain about them anywhere near as much as the

English do. The English hate their railways with a venom they otherwise reserve for horse-torturers.

England's finest moment in the Second World War was a defeat: Dunkirk, in which the British Expeditionary Force was kicked out of an ungrateful France by the Germans. This gave rise to the 'Dunkirk Spirit', which is a celebration of the way English people all pull together to achieve a disaster.

Winston Churchill summed it up for the English: 'Success consists of going from failure to failure with no loss of enthusiasm.'

3.

REFER TO 'EUROPEANS' AS IF YOU WERE FROM A DIFFERENT CONTINENT

'We generally take our holidays in Europe.' 'Have you ever been to Europe?' 'Europe is getting more expensive.' These are very English things to say. Foreign visitors are often puzzled. What continent do these people think they're from? Antarctica?

The Scots, Welsh and Irish know they are part of Europe. The Scots in particular have often allied themselves with the French against the English. But the English feel themselves to be very distinct from the other peoples of Europe. They live, in their own minds at least, in a continent unto themselves. England, as John of Gaunt puts it in Shakespeare's *Richard II*, is a 'fortress built by Nature for herself / Against infection and the hand of war.' The rest of

Europe is an *infection*, you see. Food-poisoning and rabies are only the half of it.

The greatest separation is not the Channel, but English psychology. English people believe they are essentially alone in the world, and would be downright foolish to rely on anyone else. Foreigners are inherently untrustworthy. The Germans are either at your throat or at your knees. The French and the Italians can't be relied on in a fight. The Spaniards and the Portuguese are always popping off for a siesta. The Dutch, Danes and Scandinavians will steal your wife/husband, and if television is to be believed, there are an appalling number of murders committed in their countries.

Single currency, human rights, Brussels, standardized banana lengths: these have stopped Europeans killing each other, which is all well and good. But they are not for the English.

4.

CHAMPION YOUR OWN WEATHER

When two English people meet, they first talk about the weather. Of course, this behaviour is not restricted to the English. People do this in other countries too. Where the English are different is that they believe they have the *best* weather. For the English, the weather to be found in other countries is frankly uninteresting. In southern latitudes it is monotonously hot; in Scandinavian countries it is monotonously cold; and in China or the USA they have hurricanes and earthquakes, which don't really count as weather, being more akin to the things you find in insurance policies under 'Force majeure'.

The English think they have the best weather because it is so unpredictable. 'You never know what it will do next!' Rain in June? 'Typical English summer!'

Windy April day? 'That's the beauty of English weather,' the English person will explain patiently. 'It's the variety.'

Yes, up to a point. In fact English weather is monotonous in its own way: it is monotonously clement. Bathed in the Gulf Stream, floating in its mid-latitude mediocrity, English weather, compared to the rest of the world, is mild all year round. Neither is it unpredictable. English people have been observing and measuring their weather in fine detail for the best part of 200 years, and so there is almost no weather event that hasn't a precedent: any conceivable morsel of weather is the hottest, coldest, or wettest since the 14th of August 1867.

English weather is actually quite boring, but you should never tell any English person that.

5.

BE SELF-DEPRECATING

The English are very sensitive to pomposity, solemnity or self-aggrandizement, distrusting anyone who 'puts on airs' or 'gets above themselves'. Persons caught acting in an overly self-important way are ridiculed mercilessly. When Jonathan Aitken, the former Conservative cabinet minister, was convicted in 1999 of perjury and sentenced to 18 months in prison, what made him uniquely ridiculous was that in his defence he had claimed to be wielding the 'simple sword of truth' and 'the trusty shield of fair play' against his detractors. This was very un-English. The English might believe in truth and fair play, but they never make a song and dance about it. The English are highly suspicious of high-flown rhetoric, solemn phrases, public Bible-bashing and appeals to abstract ideals, regarding them as just so much obscurantism and soft soap: and in this, their instincts are usually right.

The English can forgive hypocrisy, but rarely pretension. They are constantly at watch for it in themselves and will defend against it by putting themselves down at any opportunity. If you praise an English person's valuable antiques collection, for example, they will tell you that dusting it is the bane of their lives.

Self-deprecation is possibly a side-effect of the English class system, which is designed, through a subtle system of linguistic and behavioural shibboleths, to keep everyone in their place. As soon as the English see someone pretending to be something they're not, warning lights start flashing crimson.

6.

BE IRONIC

The English are famous for their sense of irony; that is, their propensity to say one thing and mean another. English irony is most commonly manifested in the form of understatement. For example, a foul-tasting sandwich might be described as 'somewhat lacking in the edibility department' or 'not the finest that Anglian Trains have to offer'. Occasionally (and confusingly) irony might manifest itself as hyperbole: the same horrible sandwich might be extolled as 'the very finest that Anglian Trains have to offer', which might, in fact, be both hyperbolic and true. Such utterances will often baffle foreigners, especially when delivered (as they characteristically are) in a deadpan manner. Visitors to English shores often wonder why the inhabitants seem congenitally incapable of saying what they mean.

The English are aware of their reputation for irony,

some extent have swallowed the myth that they understand it. Naturally Americans too can be ironic; so can Germans, French and Romanians (where would Eugene Ionesco have been without it?). Nevertheless the English are the only nation to have made irony a way of life. It comes out at any and every occasion, and leavens every sort of conversation, from the lightest to the most solemn. English literature is full of it, as in Jonathan Swift's *A Modest Proposal*, where he recommends that his readers eat babies.

Hold on, though, Swift was Irish, wasn't he. That's rather ironic...

7.

PLAY UP! PLAY UP! AND PLAY THE GAME!

English society is not free from corruption. There are quite regular scandals: ball-tampering in cricket, match-fixing in football, phone-hacking at newspapers and expenses-fiddling in Parliament. But the English do not accept corruption as part of life. They are still shocked and outraged each time a new scandal occurs, and demand that the malefactors be brought to justice, preferably with a long Enquiry at the taxpayers' expense. Things settle down and a new scandal comes along, followed by a new Enquiry. But the default position for the English is still that fair play – though perhaps more honoured in the breach than the observance – should be held up as the standard. Everyone deserves a 'fair chance', a 'fair crack of the whip' and a 'level playing-field'.

In English sport this sense of fair play – in which

it's not the winning, but the taking part that counts –
was perhaps best expressed by Sir Henry Newbolt in
his poem 'Vitae Lampada' (1892):

> There's a breathless hush in the Close to-night,
> Ten to make and the match to win,
> A bumping pitch and a blinding light,
> An hour to play, and the last man in.
> And it's not for the sake of a ribboned coat,
> Or the selfish hope of a season's fame,
> But his captain's hand on his shoulder smote:
> 'Play up! Play up! And play the game!'

The poem goes on to link prowess in cricket and
prowess in war. This led the poet Edith Sitwell to
comment: 'Cricket brought a great many men to their
death.'

8.

CHEER FOR THE UNDERDOG

The English don't like winners. England's greatest sporting hero is still Eddie 'the Eagle' Edwards, a ski-jumper who competed in the 1988 Winter Olympics. Mr Edwards' thick glasses constantly fogged up as he attempted the jumps, rendering the piste invisible. He came last in all his events, gaining the love and respect of his countrymen.

In more recent years the nation fell for the journalist John Sergeant, who competed on the television show *Strictly Come Dancing*. He proved so inept at the Terpsichorean art (dragging his dancing-partner supine across the floor) that he was consistently placed last by the judges; yet week after week the public voted to keep him on the show. Mr Sergeant finally resigned, saying: 'The trouble is that there is now a real danger that I might win the competition. Even for me that would be a joke too far.'

The English traditionally admire 'pluck' over skill. If someone performs with tenacity despite a lack of talent, the English instinctually feel they deserve at least as much credit as someone who performs merely well; this is a phenomenon related to the high value English place on 'playing the game' (see above). The English also prioritize humour in any social situation, and incompetence is simply more valuable, as a source of humour, than competence. And the English have pretension-phobia. They are allergic to pomposity and self-importance, and in these circumstances anyone who seems determined to make a fool of themselves is cheered as a hero.

9.

JUDGE PEOPLE AS SOON AS THEY OPEN THEIR MOUTHS

The English class system is founded, more than anything else, on the way people speak. Clipped vowels and crisply pronounced 't's at the ends of words are upper class ('rightt!', 'whott?', 'nightt nightt!'), while elongated diphthongs and glottal stops are lower class ('raigh", wo", 'nu-naigh"). The middle classes, as the name befits, fit somewhere in the middle, and are thus the object of contempt from both directions. The situation is complicated by the various regional accents and the degree to which these are either a pleasant brogue or an impenetrable bog to outsiders.

For the English, life is phonological warfare. Too 'upper' and people will assume you're looking down your nose at them; too 'lower' and people will assume you're thick or have a chip on your shoulder; too 'middle' and people will assume you're wheat-intolerant and keep llamas. A Fair Treatment at Work Survey by the Department of Trade and Industry in 2007 found that accent was cited as a cause of unfair treatment more often than sex, race or religion. And it's not just pronunciation: vocabulary also matters terribly. The most treacherous words are those that distinguish the middle classes from the upper-middles or uppers: the middles say 'pardon?', 'serviette', 'dinner', 'lounge' and 'dessert', while the uppers say 'what?', 'napkin', 'lunch', 'sitting room' and 'pudding'.

There's no escape. A homeless drunken tramp is still upper class if he speaks like an Air Vice Marshal. A plasterer who has made millions and lives in a stately home is still working class if he can't pronounce his 't's. And wherever they go and whatever they do, each will still immediately be pegged by what they call the final course of a meal.

10.

LOVE AND HATE SCOTLAND

The English love the Scots. They are a proud race, fearless, outspoken, clever and industrious. The height of English Scotomania was probably the early nineteenth century, when the novels of Walter Scott and the poetry of Robert Burns enjoyed immense popularity in England, and when the myth of the tartanclad, caber-tossing, clan-belonging Scot was created. This cult of Scotland was much tied up with the Romantic movement and the new primacy given to folk tradition, wild landscape and Celtic twilight.

However, the English also hate the Scots. They are a barbarous race, mean, weaselly, pernicious and unclean. Samuel Johnson was one of the wittiest antiCaledonians. 'The noblest prospect which a Scotsman ever sees,' he asserted, 'is the high road that leads him to England.' In his *Dictionary* he defined 'oats' as 'a grain which in England is generally given to horses, but in Scotland supports the people.' Charles Lamb –

a Romantic notwithstanding – was another. He said: 'I have been trying all my life to like Scotsmen, and am obliged to desist from the experiment in despair.' Another (there's no shortage) was the English clergyman Sydney Smith, who described Scotland as: 'That garret of the earth, the knuckle-end of England, that land of Calvin, oat-cakes and sulphur.'

These two attitudes, of Scotophilia and Scotophobia, dwell simultaneously in the soul of every English person.

The Scots themselves do not suffer from a similar schizophrenic attitude. They despise the English outright.

11.

RESIST ANY DEFINITION OF ENGLISHNESS

John Julius Norwich, the distinguished English writer and historian, said about English identity that 'what is quintessentially English is not bothering about it.' Anyone, then, who seeks to assert the existence of English characteristics is indulging in an un-English activity (which means that this book is quintessentially un-English). If he is right, we must conclude that Englishness is defined to an extent by its absence, or even more paradoxically, by its undefinability.

Why should this be? Perhaps for two reasons. Firstly, English people are temperamentally self-effacing about their national identity because in the past that identity has so ruthlessly and successfully stamped itself on the globe (the Empire, the industrial revolution, inventing all the sports, etc). Secondly,

Englishness, to the English, is always more intelligible by what is *past* – Englishness is always 'lost'; what we have in the present is always a sad falling-off from a previous state of affairs. This is quite understandable in the context of a nation that once ruled a quarter of the globe, but it runs rather deeper than that, and expresses itself in a sort of temperamental nostalgia which imbues much of English poetry, even poetry of the period when English power was at its zenith. Here the elegiac note is repeatedly struck, as in Rupert Brooke's 'The Old Vicarage, Grantchester':

> Say, is there Beauty yet to find?
> And Certainty? and Quiet kind?
> Deep meadows yet, for to forget
> The lies, and truths, and pain?… oh! yet
> Stands the Church clock at ten to three?
> And is there honey still for tea?

ENGLISH MANNERS

12.

KEEP A STIFF UPPER LIP

What is the fabled English stiff upper lip? Well, it is the capacity of the lip to resist trembling, even at moments of the highest emotion or greatest peril. The Englishman or Englishwoman should meet the intense experiences of life with nary a twitch. Or as Rudyard Kipling put it:

> If you can meet with triumph or disaster
> And treat those two imposters just the same…

…then yours is the world and everything that's in it. And what is more, you'll be a man, my son. Or a woman. You'll be English, at any rate.

As with many other things about English behaviour, there are numerous exceptions to this rule, and numerous occasions when the English let their lips go perfectly floppy. Sporting matches, award ceremonies, supermarket checkout brawls, late pizza delivery, the flattening of pets by traffic. But, more than other races – and particularly their Continental cousins – the English really do admire those who demonstrate steadfastness, self-control and humour in a tight situation, and themselves aspire to such behaviour, though they may not always achieve it. English people appreciate that not displaying emotion is not the same as not feeling emotion, and that not displaying emotion can actually, in some circumstances, be a courtesy to others. Throwing yourself onto the coffin? Certainly not. Even though Hamlet did it. But then, he was Danish.

13.

APOLOGIZE WHEN SOMEONE ELSE HAS *ALMOST* BUMPED INTO YOU, AS IF IT ACTUALLY HAPPENED, AND AS IF IT WERE YOUR FAULT

English people are often seen doing a strange dance in public places. The dance occurs, not at times of national celebration, but when two English people meet unexpectedly in a confined space such as an alleyway or towpath, or at a corner, and *almost* collide with one another.

The English are very wary of physical contact. John Donne, the English metaphysical poet, said: 'No man is an island'. While this may be true, every English person regrets the fact. So when inadvertent bodily invasion threatens, the typical English person reacts with desperate awkwardness. Both parties say 'sorry', a little under their breath, perhaps also venturing a glassy-eyed smile and looking at the ground; eye-contact is not attempted, since both parties are dreadfully embarrassed and ashamed by their mutual mealy-mouthed English flimsiness, and hesitate to catch one another's eye lest it betray something awful, reprehensible and unforgivable. Remember, no collision has actually occurred, but notwithstanding this the correct thing to do is to apologise with a sincerity that would have been appropriate had the collision actually taken place. Both parties, note, should apologize. Both should take responsibility for this non-occurring collision. This is a variant of the 'apologizing when someone has stepped on your toe' rule (see the next section), with the difference that in this case there has not been actual physical contact.

14.

APOLOGIZE WHEN SOMEONE STEPS ON YOUR TOE

The average English person apologizes around twenty times a day. At least, he or she will say 'sorry': this 'sorry', however, has a variety of meanings. It may mean 'I apologize', or it may mean 'excuse me' or it may mean 'I believe it's my turn.' Sometimes the 'sorry' may be combined with other English utterances to make a conurbation-word such as 'Sorry-Excuse-me-Thanks', which might be uttered, for example, when wishing to pass someone in a crowded train aisle.

Those twenty times add up to 7,300 apologies a year, or 613,200 in a lifetime for English women and 569,400 for English men. English women can be shown to be slightly more apologetic than English men, purely because they live longer – although the data hints that English women apologize substantially less after the age of 80, being more inclined to say things such as: 'You're in the way!'

As mentioned, the apologies that English people utter have a variety of uses. One, however, is more baffling to foreign visitors than the others. This is the apology in recognition of the fact that someone else has stepped on your foot, jostled you, or hit you on the shin with a suitcase. This is not a true apology, of course, but a small act of defiance couched as an apology, which might translate roughly as: 'You are too ill-bred to have behaved properly in public, but I am showing the way by apologizing, even though it was not my fault, and because I fear the consequences of an outright complaint, and in fact hate myself for my timidity.'

15.

FORM A QUEUE

It has been observed that an English person, left to themselves, will form an orderly queue of one. For example, at a shop counter which is temporarily unstaffed, an English person will be seen waiting patiently, facing forward, holding their purchase and vigilant to any signs that the assistant is going to return, *as if* in a queue with other people in it. They will not be seen, for example, leaning on the counter filing their nails. The posture seems to say: 'I'm next. This is the beginning of a queue even if there's only me in it, so don't try to push to the front.'

Queue-jumping is perhaps the greatest of English social sins, equalled only by asking someone how much they earn, or trying to convert them to Methodism. The queue, to the English, is the thin grey line of civilization, and represents the typically English virtues: fairness, patience, self-restraint, politeness. Violators can expect to receive the force-10 disapproval of all observers, regardless of whether or not the act of queue-jumping affects those observers personally.

In situations in which there is queue-ambiguity, for example at a ticket office with two windows where one window closes, the resulting social awkwardness is quite painful to see, because the very survival of Englishness is threatened if everyone doesn't rearrange themselves correctly. In cases like these, most English people would prefer to be magnanimous and allow someone to go ahead of them, even if they don't really deserve it, than move ahead unfairly and live with the stigma of having taken someone else's spot.

16.

DON'T MAKE ANY SUDDEN MOVEMENTS

Popular psychology would have us believe that body language reveals everything about us before we have uttered a word. Interviewers make decisions about interviewees in the first ten seconds of meeting them, and blind dates reject one another before either has stammered out a greeting.

Even if this were true, it could never apply in England. For the English, bodies don't have language, any more than cats have dictionaries. Everything about English social intercourse works to reinforce this notion. The English keep corporeal expressiveness to the bare minimum. Handshakes are brief and firm, after which arms are kept to the sides. Posture during intercourse is politely attentive but not overly so, with a buffer zone of a good two feet. The way foreigners flap their arms and hands, move their shoulders and contort their features is disturbing to the English. They feel they are being sold something, probably something with too much garlic in.

Tanks in Italy are supposed to have five reverse gears; tanks in England should have five neutral gears.

Recently the English have tended to greet one another with a little more tactility, but their hearts are not really in it. It's play-acting, and they know it. Kissing hello, hugging between men, and all the rest of the Mediterranean performance, is something they know is wrong. Such behaviour runs against notions of self-control and self-restraint, which are the hallmarks of respect for oneself and others.

17.

SAY PLEASE AND THANK YOU

As well as 'sorry' and 'excuse me', the English particularly value two other utterances: 'please' and 'thank you'.

When buying a stamp in an English post office, for example, the customer will first say 'please' when they ask for the stamp ('A first class stamp please.'). The assistant will then say 'please' when they ask for the money ("That'll be fifty pence please.'). There may be a 'thank you' from the customer as they *give* the assistant the money. There will be another 'thank you' as the money is accepted. The stamp will be passed over, possibly with an additional 'thank you', and there will be a further 'thank you' as the customer accepts the stamp. That makes two 'pleases' and four 'thank yous' just for a stamp.

This please-ing and thank you-ing doesn't mean that English people are more courteous than other races. They are simply addicted to this form of social behaviour. Saying 'please' and 'thank you', oddly, does two contradictory things at once. It creates a bond of mutual respect but also establishes a certain formal distance. 'Please' and 'thank you', if uttered in the right tone of severity, can even act as a rebuke ('I'll thank you to hand over that Holbein miniature, please.')

English people deploy 'please' and 'thank you' not so much to be polite as to remind one other that they are English.

18.

GET YOUR ROUND IN

The English pub is a place where anthropological opportunities abound. Here you can watch English people bonding or flirting with one another. You can see the uneasy ballet of aggression and restraint. You can observe the way different drinks define different people, as their cars are supposed to do. And you can see how these standards and rules become eroded as the effects of alcohol take hold.

One ritual that must be preserved, no matter how drunk the participants get, is round-buying. This is the practice whereby each drinker buys drinks for the other members of a group, usually by going to the bar, paying for the drinks, collecting them and distributing them to the other members. A drinker who 'gets his round in' (or 'her round in', although female drinkers are less likely to attach quasi-religious significance to the ritual) is looked on with approval, even if, in other respects, he is a distinctly beta- or gamma-male; a drinker who fails to do so is a pariah. Going home after having received several free drinks is behaviour that a drinker will find it very difficult to live down, and a reputation for doing so repeatedly will take years of generosity to eradicate.

One unavoidable effect of the English round-buying culture is that in a large group, say of five or more people, each drinker has to swallow quite a lot purely in order for everyone to have an opportunity to reciprocate. There is surely a PhD waiting for the first person to demonstrate a link between the round-buying culture and liver disease.

19.

BE 'DISGUSTED, TUNBRIDGE WELLS'

'Disgusted, Tunbridge Wells' is a humorous sign-off to a letter of complaint. The joke supposedly originated in the 1950s, when the editor of the *Tunbridge Wells Advertiser* found that he had nothing to put on the letters page, and commissioned an underling to write a 'letter to the editor'. The journalist signed it 'Disgusted, Tunbridge Wells' and the phrase caught on.

For the English, 'Tunbridge Wells' conjures up a very particular image. The town – it lies in west Kent and was formerly a popular spa – is considered to be the centre of 'Middle England', which is not a geographical, but a spiritual location. The inhabitants of Tunbridge Wells are characterized by their conservative (with a small 'c') opinions, their conventional tastes, their hidebound values. The typical inhabitant of Tunbridge Wells is a retired brigadier with a nicotine-stained moustache. Any threat to the established order and the moustache begins to accumulate small specks of foam. The phrase 'Disgusted, Tunbridge Wells' is thus both a celebration and a condemnation of a particular kind of Englishness.

No one would use the phrase 'Disgusted, Tunbridge Wells' except as a joke, though it is a joke that the actual residents of Tunbridge Wells no longer seem to enjoy. Some of them have suggested the phrase 'Delighted, Tunbridge Wells' as a substitute; it has garnered little interest.

20.

PRETEND IT DIDN'T HAPPEN

The opposite of the Tunbridge Wellsian tendency to carp and nitpick is the propensity to endure without complaining. English endurance is partly a result of the fabled 'stiff upper lip' (see above), but also stems from something less admirable: a temperamental fear of 'making a scene' or 'a fuss' in public. The English will endure bad behaviour, bad service, bad trains, bad food and bad haircuts without saying anything, purely because they don't want to make a public spectacle of themselves.

Why are the English so cowardly? It's difficult to say. There would appear to be a multitude of causes. The English have a class system that it is difficult to navigate, even for them, and are consequently ill at ease for much of their lives; they have to live with the enormous guilt of having dominated and despoiled a quarter of the globe, and now, post-Empire, feel somewhat shabby and pointless; they find themselves inhabiting a rather unsatisfactorily rainy island that's never really been a member of the European club. To do what other Europeans do – to shout, to gesticulate, to experiment with the emotions, to take a stand – is anathema in these circumstances. Woe betide an English person who steps out of line, gets 'above themselves' or appears 'too big for their boots', 'uppish' or 'on their high horse'. Gentle tuts will resound, and there will be dark looks and barely perceptible shakes of the head.

The English person's only defence against the bad things in life is the fabled English sense of humour, but unfortunately this is often so attenuated that it passes, neutrino-like, through all observers.

ENGLISH BEHAVIOUR

21.

CULTIVATE ECCENTRICITY

The English put a high value on eccentricity. The Eccentric Club in London, founded in 1781, once numbered the Prime Minister among its members. Currently its patron is the Duke of Edinburgh.

Many English heroes were decidedly eccentric. Take William Buckland, the nineteenth-century geologist. Buckland made it his ambition to eat every type of animal, and said that the worst-tasting were moles and bluebottles. A contemporary said this of Buckland:

> Talk of strange relics led to mention of the heart of a French King [Louis XIV] preserved at Nuneham in a silver casket. Dr. Buckland, whilst looking at it, exclaimed, 'I have eaten many strange things, but have never eaten the heart of a king before,' and, before anyone could hinder him, he had gobbled it up, and the precious relic was lost for ever.

In the long list of other contenders for Greatest English Eccentric is the writer and politician Sir George Sitwell, who tried to pay his son's fees at Eton by offering the school vegetables from his garden, and had the cows on his estate painted with willow-pattern designs to make them look more attractive. English eccentricity has always had a rather aristocratic stamp. In the modern era, the Marquess of Bath, known as 'the loins of Longleat', lives surrounded by paintings from the Kama Sutra and openly keeps a harem of 'wifelets' (mistresses) in cottages in his grounds. Among self-titled aristocrats is a former soldier called John Rothwell, who in 1986 changed his name by deed poll to King Arthur, dresses in a crown and chain-mail, carries a sword called Excalibur, and campaigns (successfully) for the rights of druids.

The English consider themselves the oddballs of Europe. To tell an English person that the Germans, Italians or Spaniards were more weird, disturbing or bizarre would be an insult.

22.

DRESS LIKE A CHAP OR CHAPPESS

The English were once among the nattiest dressers in Europe, but those days are long gone. The reality is that the average Englishman is as likely to be a T-shirted, neck-tattooed, djembe-playing crusty as anywhere else in the civilized world.

But for every action there is an equal and opposite reaction. Among the young there is a movement that seeks to counter this tide of laxity. Its adherents may be readers of *The Chap* magazine; they may identify themselves as Young Fogies; or they may simply yearn for a more tasteful, restrained and courteous age. The male of the species will typically be seen wearing tweed suits with sharp trouser-creases, brushed trilbies and shining brogues, or, if lounging by the river on a summer's afternoon, blue striped blazer and boater, a pipe clenched between manly jaws; the ladies, having said good-bye to the hairstyle known as 'the Croydon facelift' and the halter-top emblazoned with the words 'How would you like to see this on your bedroom floor?', and are now more likely to don twin-set, pearls, and stockings with conspicuous seams running down the backs (oooooh!).

For these bright young things, in short, all that stands in the way of the revolution is a good clothes brush, a trouser press, a needle and thread, and some cleaning fluid.

23.

DRESS ENTIRELY IN DEAD PEOPLE'S CLOTHING

One of the cheapest ways to dress like a chap or chappess is to visit a charity shop. Charity shops – i.e. shops that sell second-hand clothes, shoes, toys, books, etc. and donate the profits to charity – are very prominent on English high streets. Foreign visitors are often quite intrigued by them. Watch, for example, a Japanese person exploring an English charity-shop for the first time (charity shops are unknown in Japan). They can't quite believe that anyone would want to dress in other people's smelly cast-offs. Especially since much of the clothing obviously belongs to the freshly dead. Old-fashioned suits, the type where the trousers have brace-buttons and the jackets have the name of the dead person sewn into the inside pocket, are particularly well represented. In some cases, charity shops can actually be found selling used underwear. This underwear has doubtless been inspected to make sure it is irreproachable, possibly even nearly new, but it is most definitely still second-hand. Anywhere else in the developed world this would be an utterly revolting idea, like buying food that someone else has slightly nibbled on but is still actually perfectly all right.

If the foreign visitor gets over their amazement and disgust, they might 'go native' and begin spending more time in charity shops than the English themselves. Only when they go back to Tokyo wearing bespoke tailoring from a dead nonagenarian will they realize how insidious the habit has become.

24.

BARE YOUR FLESH

For those who don't wish to visit charity shops and dress up in the styles of bygone eras – and let's face it, this is the majority – the default position, especially for the young, is to bare the skin wherever possible. So, for young men, it is *de rigueur* to take the T-shirt off and bare the chest as soon as the temperature rises above 12 degrees; for the ladies, evenings will be spent revealing as much as is legally possible, even if it is Newcastle and fifteen degrees below zero, with tight micro-skirt and heels achieving the required crippled-duck gait.

Clothes were invented not just for warmth, of course, but they were invented *partly* for warmth; and so the sense of style in countries such as Italy or France will include those aspects of dress – scarves, hats, gloves, jumpers, coats – that enable the wearer to avoid freezing to death. In England these items are given the cold shoulder. They are not integrated into the overall sense of fashion, and are discarded, with joy, as if they will never be needed again, as soon as Friday or Saturday night rolls around.

Meanwhile the middle-aged and old are drabber and more covered-up in England than almost anywhere else, tending to dress in enveloping grays, browns or washed-out pastels. Clive Aslet in his book *Anyone for England?* says that 'the quintessential English garment must be the slurry-coloured waxed Barbour jacket.' True: some English men, especially among the upper classes, do seem to spend their lives trying to camouflage themselves from small animals.

25.

GO TO SLEEP IN A DECK CHAIR ON THE BEACH WEARING LOTS OF CLOTHES, BECAUSE OF THE COLD

The exception to the 'bare your flesh' rule is at the beach, where the year-round freezing wind makes adequate clothing essential; and, since English people don't tend to go to the beach on a Friday or Saturday night, there is no need to take one's clothes off (the English prefer not to swim in their own country). English people will therefore tend to be more warmly dressed at Skegness or Scarborough than they would anywhere else. They will also be determined to have a good time, and since having a good time means staring at the sea as if it were a broken television set, a deckchair is needed. The combination of immobility, warm clothing and a heavy seaside lunch (fish and chips, doughnuts, beer) promotes sleep. Thus is the typical English holidaymaker revealed. Swaddled as if in retreat from Moscow circa 1943, dribbling slightly, with a painfully full bladder, dreaming of being on holiday in Greece.

King Canute is said to have positioned himself at the sea's edge and commanded the waves to retreat. Sometimes it seems as if a collective act of will is taking place, and the massed ranks of bundled-up English holidaymakers are responsible for the outgoing tides.

26.

SHOW VISITORS YOUR AIRING CUPBOARD

England is notable for its very high levels of home ownership. In England, 70% of houses are 'owned' by their occupants (in reality, they often rent them from a mortgage company, but that is a technical point), compared to, for example, 55% in France and a mere 42% in Germany. This gives rise to some characteristic English behaviour. English people spend an immoderate amount of time on Do-It-Yourself activities, happily gutting kitchens and knocking through walls, with 22% of accident and emergency admissions being DIY-related. The English are also obsessed with house prices, interest rates and mortgage products, and these subjects may fill the entirety of a dull English evening's conversation.

The pride and sense of ownership that English

people feel in relation to their houses is expressed in 'the tour' that they will offer new visitors to a house, especially a house that has just been done up with some judicious gutting. On 'the tour', guests are conducted through the rooms, usually by the woman of the house, who will keep up a running commentary on the deficiencies of the property (for modesty's sake), the work that has been done to bring it into the modern age, and any acceptable relics of a previous age (exposed beams, dado rails). The various conveniences will not be neglected, including the bathroom, toilets, under-stairs cupboard 'where the vacuum cleaner lives' and in extreme cases, the airing cupboard. There is nothing sensible that can possibly said about an airing cupboard, and so this is the point where both visitor and host will feel slightly absurd.

27.

BUY A GNOME

A gnome is a garden ornament featuring a little rosy-faced man (or sometimes woman) wearing a pointed hat. He may be fishing, pushing a wheelbarrow or baring his buttocks (a 'mooning gnome'). Gnomes are much beloved of the English. The link between gnomes and Christmas is an interesting one: gnomes, like the rest of the Christmas icons (Santa, reindeer, sleigh, elves), are an import from Europe, and, like the Christmas icons, appear commonly as garden ornaments. Yet whereas the Christmas icons obviously appear only at Christmas, the gnome is all-year-round. Gnomes are Santa's unhelpful helpers: bad-tempered, anarchic elves. They are Christmas defectors.

Gnomes are semiologically complex. They signify, first and foremost, a shocking lack of taste. They are rather like the Vladimir Tretchikoff pictures of green-faced women that used to hang over the mantelpieces of English homes in the 1960s and 70s. They may also signify that the gnome-owner is aware that they signify a shocking lack of taste and doesn't care; and perhaps, in fact, is consciously cultivating an image as an eccentric, though without much originality or daring or indeed eccentricity.

It remains a curious fact that although gnomes are associated with lower- and middle-class gardens, they have an upper-class pedigree: the first gnomes were imported by Sir Charles Isham, 10th Baronet of Lamport, in 1874, who filled his home, Lamport Hall in Northamptonshire, with them.

In recent years 'gnome liberationists' have received much media attention. These people steal gnomes from gardens in order to return them to the wild, which often means taking them on holiday and sending their former owners photos of them at Machu Picchu.

28.

SIT IN A COTTAGE GARDEN FULL OF HOLLYHOCKS

There's an odd moment in the Second-World-War film *The Wooden Horse*. An English airman who has escaped from a German prison camp is captured by the French Resistance, who suspect that he is a spy. They interrogate him to see whether he is truly English. The crucial question is: 'What kind of flowers are in your mother's garden?' The Englishman knows immediately. 'Roses, lupins, pansies, geraniums,' he says.

A modern English airman might not have this information so closely to hand. Nevertheless there is still something very English about a cottage garden full of flowers.

Cottage gardens originated in England in the Elizabethan period. As time went on they began to be attached to larger and grander properties; not just cottages, but stately homes. The English cottage garden tends above all to be informal. It mixes flowers with herbs, vegetables and fruit trees. The planting tends to be dense, often in great massed banks, and there is a sense of ordered disorder. Scattered throughout the garden will be various architectural elements: benches, sundials, topiary, statues. Typical plants will include daisies, hollyhocks, foxgloves, peonies, delphiniums, wisteria, as well as the roses, lupins, pansies and geraniums favoured by the mothers of escaping POWs.

There is something very English about sitting in the mild sunshine surrounded by hollyhocks, perhaps with a cup of tea on one's lap in which a wasp is slowly drowning, and going into a drowse. A good drowse simply cannot be achieved in the highly planned and geometrical gardens found elsewhere in Europe.

29.

RETREAT TO YOUR SHED

Proverbially, the Englishman's home is his castle. However, it would be more accurate to say that the Englishman's garden shed is his castle. The Englishman's home, after all, generally contains an Englishwoman, and, too often, some English children, which may make it impossible to exercise sovereignty.

What is a shed? It's a place to withdraw, where an Englishman can tinker with things, brew beer, make tea on a camping stove, smoke cigarettes (especially if he is not allowed to do so in the house or his wife thinks he has given up), hoard old newspapers or suggestive pieces of wood or metal, or keep chickens he has killed himself, because his wife won't allow them in her freezer.

'Why not? It's just a chicken.'

'It's not the same, is it?'

'It's exactly the same.'

'Well I don't care, I'm not having it in the house.'

The shed may become such a focus of an Englishman's life that he begins to devote time and attention to Doing It Up in the style of a Roman temple or a pirate galley. This is when things have probably Gone Too Far and the marriage is approaching a crisis. If his wife leaves him, the Englishman will have the perfect place in which to sit and wonder where it has All Gone Wrong.

ENGLISH
ENTERTAINMENTS

VISIT THE V&A

30.

VISIT THE V&A

This section is called 'English entertainments' rather than 'English culture': the English are naturally suspicious of culture. Few English people know anything about their greatest contemporary writers, painters, sculptors, dancers, poets and singers, feeling safe in the knowledge that they will be there when they need them, probably in their old age – like Radio Three.

The exception to the general distrust of culture is museum-going. London, Bristol, Norwich, Leeds, Birmingham, Manchester and other cities boast fine museums, many of them free, and all of them well attended, not just by tourists, but by the English themselves. Perhaps London's greatest museum is the Victoria and Albert (the V&A), located in the 'Albertopolis' of South Kensington (a district that also takes in the Science Museum and the Natural

History Museum). The V&A is the world's largest museum of decorative arts and culture, containing 4.5 million objects from around the world, and spanning five millennia. Among its holdings are costumes, glassware, sculpture, paintings, metalwork, tapestry, books, furniture, photographs, drawings and much, much more. There is also a department devoted to performance, in which items representing rock, pop, ballet, drama, circus and music hall are displayed.

The impression is not so much a museum as a celebration of human endeavour and expression since the dawn of time.

31.

GO TO THE NOTTING HILL CARNIVAL

London's Notting Hill Carnival is held every year in August. It is the second-largest carnival in the world after the Rio Carnival, and attracts well over a million people.

It began in 1959 as a response to racial violence. A series of racist attacks had led to rioting, and the staff of a small London newspaper, the *West Indian Gazette*, decided to do something about it. 'We needed something to get the taste of Notting Hill out of our mouths,' the editor, Claudia Jones, said. She invited the various ethnic minority groups of Notting Hill – not just West Indians, but Irish, Ukrainians, Portuguese and Africans – to join in a festival. It took place indoors, since the idea of a street carnival in late 1950s England seemed completely absurd. But as the idea gathered momentum, organizers borrowed floats from the fire brigade, costumes from Madame Tussaud's, and horses and carts from stallholders in the Portobello market, and took to the streets. It became part political demonstration, part act of defiance, part cultural celebration.

Nowadays the festival has a predominantly Caribbean flavour, without much in the way of Ukrainian or Irish. There is curried goat and rum punch; calypso musicians in pork-pie hats; women in extravagant sequined and feathered costumes; and the inevitable policemen attempting dance-steps with half-naked revellers. Enormous in scale, anarchic in essence, unquenchable in spirit, the carnival has become a firmly established part of English cultural life.

32.

VISIT GLYNDEBOURNE

Rather different, but equally English, is Glyndebourne, an English country house near Lewes, Sussex, about 50 miles south of London. It stages an annual opera festival that is a staple of the English Summer Social Season (this being a round of enjoyments for the social elite that includes events such as Henley Royal Regatta, Goodwood and Wimbledon). The Glyndebourne Festival is particularly noted for its productions of Mozart operas, but it also stages works by composers as diverse as Gershwin and Janáček.

Because Glyndebourne has traditionally been associated with the upper classes, it retains an image as a playground for rich people who have no particular interest in opera and are more interested in having picnics on the lawns and getting drunk. And indeed Glyndebourne continues to enforce certain traditional standards of dress (black tie for men and flowery dresses for ladies). The picnic element continues to be an important part of the whole experience. The intervals of the performances are specially extended to allow time for the audience to treat themselves adequately to game pie, Pimms (a gin-based drink) and strawberry tart.

It would be a mistake, though, to see Glyndebourne as merely a junket for the well-bred. Glyndebourne is now much involved in educational programmes, and has a world-renowned touring company. The festival has been championed by some unlikely figures. Jeanette Winterson, a novelist not well known for taking southern twits seriously, said of Glyndebourne: 'Every time you come here you're in for a shock', which was presumably a comment on the daring stage-sets and ground-breaking productions rather than a reference to the exorbitant ticket prices.

33.

GO TO THE PROMS

The annual Promenade concerts ('the Proms') in London are a cheaper option than Glyndebourne. These classical music recitals, founded by Sir Henry Wood in 1895, take place over eight weeks in summer, mainly at the Royal Albert Hall in South Kensington. 'Promenade' refers to the fact that audience members stand while listening. For each concert there are more than a thousand of these standing places available, at a price of £5 per ticket. These cannot be bought in advance, and so the only way to get one is to queue up beforehand.

The most famous concert in the proms season is the Last Night of the Proms, which takes place in mid-September. The Last Night is traditionally performed in a jocular atmosphere: the conductor gives a funny speech, and the audience wave flags and wear T-shirts with slogans such as 'Henry Wood Did it Standing

Up'. The same pieces are always played: Elgar's *Pomp and Circumstance March* (which includes the tune 'Land of Hope and Glory'); 'Rule Britannia', a song asserting Britannia's dominion over the seas; the National Anthem, which expresses the wish that the Queen conquer her enemies; and the musical setting of William Blake's 'Jerusalem' (see below), which longs for the return of Jesus Christ to England's 'green and pleasant land'. The whole experience is an orgy of English nationalism that finds almost no other outlet during the rest of the year (see 'Stop at a St George's Cross motorway burger stand', below) and is enormously popular, being relayed on giant screens to thousands of cheering part-time nationalists in Hyde Park.

34.

WATCH CORONATION STREET

Coronation Street is the world's longest-running TV soap opera. It is set in the fictional town of Weatherfield, supposedly somewhere in Greater Manchester. It was first broadcast in 1960, when the idea of a TV show featuring the lives of ordinary working-class people was a novelty. At first it came under much suspicion for its use of Northern dialect words such as 'nowt' (meaning nothing), 'keks' (meaning clothes) and 'our kid' (meaning a sibling or friend), and the *Daily Mirror* pronounced that it would not last more than three weeks. It is now a national institution. Rather astonishingly, it still features two of the actors that were in the first series: William Roache and Philip Lowrie.

In the 1990s the programme came under a rather different criticism, that of not being realistic enough, at least in comparison to newer soap operas such as *Brookside* and *East Enders*. *Coronation Street* consequently underwent a revamp, introducing storylines that focussed on 'issues' such as drug abuse, homosexuality, environmental activism, religious cults, internet chat room abduction, cancer and transsexualism. But even these sensational improvements paled beside the infamous 50-year anniversary extravaganza of 2010. In this, a local bar exploded during a party, destroying a viaduct, and causing a tram to run into the street and engulf much of the set in a ball of flame. Three characters were killed outright and one was trapped in the ruins of her burnt-out shop; meanwhile another character gave birth prematurely after her husband took a hammer to a woman who had been stalking him, and two more got married in an emergency ward, only for the groom to go into cardiac arrest.

35.

WATCH AN EALING COMEDY

The films known as Ealing Comedies were produced by Ealing Studios in London between about 1947 and 1957. Because of this comparatively narrow time-span, the Ealing Comedies give a remarkable snapshot of a particular period of English history. The Second World War had just ended (the Comedies are full of bombed-out buildings); there is still food rationing; an army of spivs and ne'er-do-wells seeks to profit from the post-war upheaval; English social and sexual mores are changing; and there are radical new developments in science and technology.

But what makes the Ealing Comedies most significant is that they are gloriously funny. They are also superbly written and directed, and wonderfully shot in black and white, being among the last monochrome films to be made in England. They saw the emergence of a cadre of actors who went on to become famous in the post-war years, including Alastair Sim, Peter Sellers, Alec Guinness and Joan Greenwood.

Among the best Ealing Comedies are *Kind Hearts and Coronets* (1949), about a minor member of an aristocratic family who commits eight murders in order to become the head of his clan; *Passport to Pimlico* (1949), about a group of Londoners who try to set up an independent republic; *The Man in the White Suit* (1951), about an inventor who produces a white cloth that never stains; *The Lavender Hill Mob* (1951), about a mild-mannered bank clerk who executes a daring gold robbery; *The Titfield Thunderbolt* (1953) about a group of villagers who try to save their railway branch line from government cuts; and *The Ladykillers* (1955), about a gang of incompetent criminals who are foiled by an old lady.

36.

SEE A PUNCH AND JUDY SHOW

Punch and Judy puppet shows were introduced into England from Italy at some time in the 16th century. The stock characters are the hook-nosed, stick-brandishing Mr Punch; his long-suffering wife Judy; their even-more-long-suffering baby; a policeman; a crocodile; a hangman; a devil; and a doctor. A long string of sausages inevitably makes an appearance. Performances are carried out in a raised box, sides covered in a red-and-white striped cloth. The puppet-master inside the box is known as a 'professor' and the characteristic gleeful squawk of Mr Punch (*'That's* the way to do it!') is produced by means of a reed device known as a 'swazzle'.

There is nothing politically correct about Mr Punch. He beats his wife, sits on his baby, outwits the police –

he even wins against the devil. Charles Dickens called him 'one of those extravagant reliefs from the realities of life which would lose its hold upon the people if it were made moral and instructive.'

Mr Punch has often been used to symbolize the English, and the humorous magazine *Punch* – which ran from 1841 to 2002 – was named after him. Essentially, Mr Punch is how the English would like to see themselves: anarchic, irrepressible, able to surrender themselves to their appetites. The fact that most of the time they are so obviously *not* these things is why Mr Punch is so perennially popular, and why he often appears at the seaside, that zone where the rules of everyday life can temporarily be overturned.

37.

LISTEN TO THE SHIPPING FORECAST

The shipping forecast is a weather forecast for the benefit of sailors, broadcast four times a day on BBC Radio.

Many more people listen to it on land than at sea. Hundreds of thousands listen to the late-night broadcast on Radio 4 at 12:48 am, despite the fact they are more in danger of spilling cocoa on themselves than being pounded by giant waves.

'Dogger, Fisher, German Bight. Southwest veering southeast 3 or 4, occasionally 5 later. Rain, then squally showers. Moderate, becoming poor.' And so it goes on. Most of the listeners are not quite sure what it means. But they know there is real and present danger out there at sea: they know that mariners are hearkening keenly to this information and writing it down. There is the same sort of vicarious thrill that one might derive from listening to police radio.

The paradox of the shipping forecast is that it is almost mathematically precise and practical, and yet has an eerie poetry: 'Low Forties 976 losing its identity. Low Southern England 975 expected Northern Germany 996 by midday tomorrow. Atlantic high moving slowly northeast, expected South Fitzroy 1032 by same time.' For the English, the shipping forecast expresses something about the national character; or, perhaps more accurately, about how they would like the national character to be seen. It is measured, restrained, decent, rational, subtle. As it works its way through the sea areas, listeners are reminded that they live on an island, separate from Europe. The shipping forecast surrounds them, contains them, defines them.

38.

GO TO A FINGER-IN-THE-EAR FOLK PERFORMANCE AND JOIN IN THE CHORUS

Folk music is one of the few arenas of English life in which it is normal and permissible for an English person to describe themselves as 'English' rather than 'British'. English folk music originated from a time when England was not joined politically with Wales, Scotland and Ireland. It's entirely natural, therefore, for audiences at modern-day folk concerts to consider themselves, temporarily, sons and daughters of the land, outlaws of Robin Hood's band, happy medieval peasants drinking a pint of English ale after a hard day's winnowing. And there's nothing quite like a sea shanty for urbanites who would feel sea-sick in a canoe.

Folk music is currently undergoing a revival in

England. There are hundreds of folk festivals every year, and countless folk clubs and recitals in village halls and in the upstairs rooms of pubs. Traditional instruments include melodeons, mandolins, harps, recorders, flutes and lutes; there is fusion funk played on Hang drums and didgeridoos; and spin-offs including electric folk, folk punk and folk metal. The new wave of English folk performers includes international stars such as Eliza Carthy, Billy Bragg, Nancy Kerr, Seth Lakeman and Kathryn Tickell.

Performers, especially in the more solemn circles, tend to exhibit a characteristic nasal vocal style that sounds as if they are straining painfully to achieve the correct pitch and failing, a habit sometimes accompanied by cupping the ear or pressing the temple in concentration. Some folk musicians really don't do themselves any favours.

ENGLISH CRIMES

39.

RIOT

39.

RIOT

The 2011 riots were not British riots but English riots. They occurred in London, Bristol, Birmingham, Manchester and Liverpool. They echoed previous English riots: the Gordon riots of 1780, the Priestley Riots of 1791, the Luddite Riots of 1811-12, the Bristol Riots of 1831, the Luton 'Peace Day' Riots of 1919 (during which rioters broker into a music shop to loot pianos, singing 'Keep the Home Fires Burning'), the Notting Hill Riots of 1958, the Southall Riots of 1979, the Brixton, Toxteth and Handsworth Riots of 1981 (a bumper year), the Broadwater Farm Riot of 1985, the Poll Tax Riots of 1990, the Oldham Riots of 2001, and the Birmingham Riots of 2005. During this time Scotland, Wales and Northern Ireland were comparatively quiescent.

Some of these riots were religious, some political, and some racial in origin. The 2011 riots had no obvious origin: some commentators blamed social exclusion, others gang culture, criminal opportunism, the breakdown of family values, materialism, moral anarchy and the failure of policing (the riots began after the shooting of a young man in a police raid). Any and all of these theories might have been valid, but the riots also had roots in peculiarly English attitudes. The English do not like being governed. They tend to see politicians as venal ('They're All on the Take'), dislike officials and those in uniform ('Jobsworths') and generally view the instruments of state with contempt ('All Coppers are Bastards'). These attitudes, if allowed to fester, occasionally tip over into civil unrest.

After the riots in 2011, 'love walls' were created in many of the affected areas. These too were a purely English phenomenon. They consisted of walls covered with hundreds of multicoloured post-it notes with slogans on them such as: 'Stop burning my city', 'This is our home' and 'Peckham 4Ever'.

40.

ACT LIKE A HOOLIGAN

In foreign countries, the English are known by two stereotypes: the English gentleman and the English football hooligan. The English gentleman dresses in tweed suit, trilby and monocle, is unfailingly polite at all times, and goes out of his way to help ladies, children and small animals. The English football hooligan dresses in Paisley and steel toe-capped boots, is unfailingly drunk and obnoxious at all times, and goes out of his way to commit grievous bodily harm while chanting obscenities and hurling small objects at the referee.

It's a very strange situation. No other nation has a public image so sharply polarized. Some have argued that the two stereotypes are in fact two sides of the same coin, i.e. that English restraint/politeness and English obnoxiousness/violence spring from the same cause. The anthropologist Kate Fox put it this way: 'Both tendencies reflect a fundamental and distinctively English social dis-ease, a chronic and seemingly incurable inability to engage normally and directly with other human beings.'

So English hooligans behave in the way they do because they feel socially awkward and are unable to communicate. Perhaps this is true, and football hooligans just need to be understood. In 2006 the then Leader of the Opposition, David Cameron, got into trouble by suggesting just this, i.e. that 'hoodies' (young men wearing hooded tops, often blamed for crime) just needed 'a lot more love' to make them into responsible citizens. This was ridiculed as his 'hug-a-hoodie' policy and nearly sank his attempt to become Prime Minister.

41.

GO ON A COUNTRY HOUSE MURDER WEEKEND

The English are very great lovers of murder. They consume enormous quantities of it, often in the form of television programmes such as *Midsummer Murders* or *Poirot*.

However, there are always those whose love of killing is not sated by these entertainments. For them there is the country house murder weekend.

In a typical event the participants are presented with a murdered body and must exercise their wits by discovering 'whodunnit'. They interact with actors playing the various suspects, and quiz them about their movements and motives. It's rather like 'Cluedo' only with real people. Mrs Peacock in the ballroom with a spanner? Colonel Mustard in the jacuzzi with a Kalashnikoff?

Some newer forms of murder mystery involve grittier plots – as consumed in vast quantities in novels and films – in which people are abducted, hung up in basements and tortured, or buried alive and taunted through tubes. Real police officers may play parts as actors or consultants.

Murder events have proliferated past the 'country house weekend' setting and can be organized for hen parties, birthdays, even for Christmas, when the thing in the chimney is not Santa but a dismembered corpse.

42.

SUCCUMB TO THE ENGLISH VICE

'The English vice' is actually a translation from the French. It seems that in the 19th century the French were appalled by the prevalence of corporal punishment in British public schools, and so labelled any kind of flagellation (caning, whipping, slippering, beating) 'le vice Anglais'. Later this came to have sadomasochistic sexual connotations.

There is no real evidence that flagellation is any more prevalent in England than in other countries of the world, but the English take enthusiastically to the stereotype. The reasons are twofold. Firstly, the English find the very idea of 'buttocks' hilarious. Secondly, the English know that their global reputation for sexual prowess is zero, and so anything that makes them seem a little perverted and dangerous is to be welcomed. Thus the fame of 'Miss Whiplash', aka Lindi St Clair, England's most famous prostitute, who earned enough money servicing Members of Parliament to buy a bright pink Rolls Royce.

As well as 'the English vice' there is 'the English disease'. 'The English disease', unlike 'the English vice', has nothing to do with flagellation. It is a sobriquet awarded to the English by the English themselves. It refers simply to any undesirable social trend. Football hooliganism, late trains, obesity, alcohol misuse, hypocrisy, are all regularly labelled 'the English disease'. 'The English disease', in fact, is whatever the English wish to have a good moan about. Perhaps the need to have a good moan is the real English disease.

43.

OBSESS OVER LORD LUCAN

'Lord Lucan' was Richard John Bingham, 7th Earl of Lucan, a British peer, who disappeared on the night of 8 November 1974 following the murder of his children's nanny, Sandra Rivett. It has been assumed that he was involved in some way with the nanny's killing (she was found in the cellar in a bloodstained sack): some think that he meant to kill his wife, Lady Lucan, and mistook the nanny for the wife.

Since 1974 Lord Lucan has been the focus of enormous media interest and has been spotted in several locations around the world, including India, Africa and Australia, but never with any degree of certainty. There have been numerous books claiming to give the definitive solution to the mystery, all of which contradict one another, and his story has featured in novels, television programmes and films. He was pronounced officially dead in 1999.

The English obsession with Lord Lucan is partly to do with the English love of anything aristocratic (Lucan had a gambling playboy lifestyle, killed a nanny, and was later seen in various mouldering parts of the British Empire) but also because Lucan 'got away with it', something that the English wholeheartedly approve of. A working-class parallel had been played out just a few years earlier by the Great Train Robber Ronnie Biggs, who fled from justice to South America, and was widely supported by the English public.

In humorous conversation, Lord Lucan is a sort of shorthand for anyone mysterious or anything unexplained. If an unknown person appears in a wedding photograph, for example, a wit might ask: 'Is that Lord Lucan?'

44.

HAVE SEX AT 15

The legal age of consent to sexual relations in England is 16. Despite this, the under-16 conception rate is the highest in Western Europe. In England, girls get pregnant earlier than they do in France, Spain (where the age of consent is 13), Germany, Italy, Portugal, Holland (Holland!), Liechtenstein, and everywhere else. The teenage pregnancy rate in England is fourteen times higher than it is in South Korea.

What could possibly be the cause?

Many explanations have been put forward. The dysfunctional English attitude to alcohol has been fingered; also the lack of adequate contraception provision, the low socio-economic status of many young mothers, the benefits culture, the sexualization of children in the media, and so on.

One that is rarely explored is the English temperament. It is antipathetic to law. No English person likes legislation, and politicians are regularly heard saying that there is 'too much of it'. Even the constitution is unwritten. The English have nothing but contempt for 'health and safety', 'political correctness' and other codes, written or unwritten, that tell them what to do and how to think. English boys and girls imbibe this attitude to authority with their (teenage) mothers' milk, and as soon as they get the chance to break the law, they do, in the most natural way possible.

This probably doesn't mean that the best way to get an English 15-year-old into bed is engage them in a debate on the English constitution.

45.

GO ON A JACK THE RIPPER TOUR

Jack the Ripper was the unknown murderer who killed and mutilated a series of women, mostly prostitutes, in the Whitechapel district of London's East End from 1888 to 1891. The victim count varies from five to eleven. Jack, known at the time as 'the Whitechapel Murderer' or 'Leather Apron', taunted the police in a series of letters, one of which contained half a human kidney. Because the internal organs of some of the victims were removed, suspicion fell on surgeons, butchers and animal slaughterers. To date, there have been hundreds of theories on the identity of the culprit. Even Queen Victoria had a theory: the murderer, she felt, could have been a worker on a cattle-boat moored at London's docks. Others suspected Prince Eddy, Victoria's grandson. In fact, there are few people alive at the time who have *not* at some time been the object of suspicion, including Arthur Conan Doyle and Oscar Wilde.

The East End milieu of the crimes, the association with prostitution and the aristocracy, gaslight, cobbled streets and hansom cabs, have combined to create a unique aura around these terrible crimes. Ripper enthusiasts form a community and have dignified themselves with the name 'Ripperologists'. There are Ripper walking tours in the heart of Jack the Ripper's Old London Town, during which fans can see the original locations, be thrilled by the sex and violence, and speculate on the candidates. One tour offers customers hand-held projectors featuring 'RipperVision'™, in which grisly images of mutilated corpses are displayed.

Some feel this is all in rather poor taste. They are right.

46.

VISIT BAKER STREET

If anyone could have helped in the matter of the Whitechapel murders, it would have been Sherlock Holmes, who lived, as we know, at 221b Baker Street. Visitors to this address are greeted by a sign saying: 'Sherlock Holmes Museum: Sherlock Holmes and Doctor Watson lived at 221b Baker Street between 1881-1904, according to the stories written by Sir Arthur Conan Doyle.' This leaves some room for the possibility that Conan Doyle was a figment of Sherlock Holmes's imagination rather than the other way round.

At the museum there is everything one might expect. Meerschaum pipes, penny-post letters, a violin, a microscope, a Bunsen burner, some Pall Mall Turkish cigarettes No.3, a phrenological head, a display of the contents of the pockets of an Indonesian seaman circa 1892, a life-size waxwork of a Baker Street

Irregular... and then there is the gift shop, preserved as it would have been in Sherlock Holmes's day, with silver figurines of Sherlock Holmes, Sherlock Holmes magnifying glasses, Sherlock Holmes fridge magnets, Sherlock Holmes teapots, Sherlock Holmes tea-sets, Sherlock Holmes candles, Sherlock Holmes statues, Sherlock Holmes pens, Sherlock Holmes chess-sets, Sherlock Holmes friezes, Sherlock Holmes keyrings, Sherlock Holmes USB sticks, and signs that say 'Please adjust your dress before leaving'.

Did Sherlock Holmes really exist? Well, that is a three-pipe problem. Hand me that tin of shag, Watson...

ENGLISH LANGUAGE

47.

BE NICE

Imagine a discussion about holidays at an English hairdresser:

'How was the food?'
'Nice!'
'What was the weather like?'
'Nice!'
'What was the hotel like?'
'Nice!'
'What were the people like?'
'Nice!'
'What were the blokes like?'
'Nice!'
'What were the beaches like?'
'Nice!'

The real answers are, in order, overpriced, torrid,

purulent, ingratiating, monomaniacal and condom-infested, but English people prefer not to deploy any of the words available to them in the 20 volumes of the Oxford English Dictionary, and instead use the all-purpose word 'nice', presumably in case any alternative is perceived as 'not nice', i.e. not friendly, accommodating or normal.

Perusal of the famous dictionary will reveal that 'nice' has 44 different meanings, some historical, but many in current usage. These latter include 'well-executed' ('Nice one!'), kind ('That was nice of you'), sexually attractive ('Nice arse!'), respectable ('a girl from a nice family'), full and satisfying ('I could do with a nice dinner'), difficult to decide or settle ('It's a nice question'), exhibiting good behaviour ('Eating out of dustbins is not nice') and scrupulous ('We can't afford to be too nice in our methods').

In some cases these meanings can be conflated. For example, eating out of dustbins is not good behaviour, and neither is it very sexually attractive.

48.

BE PARLIAMENTARY

Westminster has spawned a number of intriguing linguistic usages. One is that Members of Parliament (MPs) must never refer to each other by their own names. An MP called Jane Smith, for example, who was elected in Newton Abbott, becomes 'the Honourable Member for Newton Abbott'. Similarly it is forbidden for MPs in the House of Commons to refer to the House of Lords. This should be called 'the other place' or 'another place', as if the speaker were suffering an attack of amnesia. Members of the House of Lords must similarly refer to the House of Commons as 'the other place' or 'another place'; although, in this case, amnesia might be to blame.

In fact, Parliament is often more notable for what members can't say than what they can. MPs may not suggest that another MP has false motives or is drunk or lying; neither may they misrepresent what another

MP has said or use any language deemed to be insulting or abusive. This last prohibition has led to some rich comedy over the years. Among the epithets that MPs have been forced to withdraw are 'fat bounder', 'slanderer', 'murderer', 'bastard', 'jackass', 'cheeky young pup', 'squirt', 'dimwit', 'cheat', 'crook', 'coward', 'guttersnipe', 'Pharisee', 'hooligan', 'pipsqueak', 'stool-pigeon', 'rat', 'swine' and 'member returned by the refuse of a large constituency'. Insults in the House of Commons are rather like sins in the Catholic confessional. As long the MP immediately withdraws the remark, he or she can get away with anything.

Some MPs have taken an ironic delight in concealing their insults. Notable alternatives for 'lie' have included 'terminological inexactitude' and 'economical with the truth', both of which phrases have entered the English language.

49.

READ PRIVATE EYE

Private Eye is a satirical magazine established by a group of friends at Shrewsbury School, an English public school, in the late 1950s. It now sells nearly a quarter of a million copies per issue. The magazine is a mixture of humour and campaigning journalism, dedicated to exposing the pretensions, incompetence and corruption of the powerful and celebrated – a very English activity – and as a result is constantly being sued for libel. For first-time readers it is sometimes difficult to see what is intended to be serious in the magazine and what is not. This deliberate ironizing is also very English.

Many of the in-jokes of the magazine have entered the language. Someone who is taking part in 'Ugandan discussions' is having (usually illicit) sexual intercourse. Someone who is 'tired and emotional' is drunk. 'Brenda' is Her Majesty the Queen. The *Eye*'s fake columnists are well known: feature writer Glenda Slagg; Trotskyist political commentator Dave Spart; tired-and-emotional hack journalist Lunchtime O'Booze; sports columnist Sally Jockstrap; and current affairs columnist Mary Ann Bighead. The editor is the fictional 'Lord Gnome', and the 'Curse of Gnome' is imagined to fall on anyone who crosses swords with the magazine and then suffers a personal misfortune.

Private Eye magazine is quintessentially English, having its origins in the English public-school system and Oxbridge, with English upper-middle-class editors, and concerning itself chiefly with English politicians and personalities; and so despite its UK-wide availability it is not in any real sense a 'British' publication.

50.

WRITE A CLERIHEW

This is a clerihew:

> Jonathan Swift
> Never went up in a lift.
> Neither did Robinson Crusoe
> Do so.

The form can be described as a four-line verse containing two rhyming couplets of irregular length and scansion. It was invented around 1900 by the sixteen-year-old Edmund Clerihew Bentley as a way of relieving the boredom of school lessons, and has since been widely practised and imitated.

Most clerihews are biographical in nature, taking a famous person as their subject. One of the few that isn't, takes the topic of biography itself as a subject:

> The art of Biography

Is different from Geography.
Geography is about maps,
But Biography is about chaps.

Bentley published three collections of clerihews, in 1905, 1929 and 1939. The form was also practised by the English humorist GK Chesterton, who was a school-friend of Bentley.

The clerihew is a distinctly English poetic form. It reduces entire careers to the size of a postage stamp, and does it in a way that is frankly inelegant. Yet clerihews are rarely mocking or satirical. True clerihews tend, above all, to be silly, and the English love things that are silly.

It only irritated Brahms
To tickle him under the arms.
What really helped him to compose
Was to be stroked on the nose.

51.

BROWSE IN CHARING CROSS ROAD

If a foreign visitor happens to be in Wales and admits to a love of second-hand books, he will be directed to Hay-on-Wye. If that same visitor is in London, he will be directed to Charing Cross Road. Starting from Tottenham Court Road tube station and heading south towards Trafalgar Square, the area, comprising Charing Cross Road and Cecil Court, is home to dozens of bookshops: children's bookshops, theatre bookshops, Italian and Chinese bookshops, dance bookshops, antiquarian bookshops, science fiction bookshops, and many more.

Brooding over them all is the vast and magisterial presence of Foyles, once the biggest bookshop in the world. Founded in 1903, Foyles was famous for its refusal to make any concession to the convenience of the modern customer. Anyone wishing to buy a book had to queue three times: once to get a 'chit' (an invoice) for the book; once to pay at a kiosk where transactions were slowly carried out without the benefit of cash registers; and once to collect the book itself, from an assistant who often seemed to let you have it as a favour. The books tended to be shelved by publisher rather than by subject, making them impossible to find, though in many cases they were not shelved at all, remaining in dusty heaps on the floor (which was irritating, since you had to queue around them). One wit remarked that the experience was rather as if Kafka had gone into the book trade. Nevertheless Foyles thrived on its reputation as the nexus of a particularly English disdain for business, or, more accurately, the way everyone else did business. Nowadays, of course, Foyles has been changed and modernized out of all recognition. Perhaps you even bought this book at Foyles. In the past this would have been difficult.

52.

FAIL TO LEARN ANY LANGUAGES

The number of languages spoken by the average world citizen is three: a purely local language or dialect, a national language, and a colonial language (often English, French or Spanish).

The average number of languages spoken by English people is one. English. Most English people learn a language at school – French, German, Spanish – but they don't take it seriously. The reason is not hard to see. Everyone, everywhere in the world, speaks English. The Germans speak it with a barely concealed contempt, the Dutch speak it literally better than the English themselves (and with what sounds like a perverted relish) and the Japanese speak English by virtue of the fact that 20% of their language is made up of English loan-words (making Japanese one of the easiest, rather than the hardest, languages for an English person to learn). English is the world's *lingua franca*, the official language of the European Union and the language of international communication and diplomacy. So why bother?

Naturally, English people know that they are lucky to be blessed with this state of affairs, and are secretly a little ashamed of their laziness. But they console themselves with the thought that English is easy to learn, and so Johnny Foreigner doesn't deserve much credit for his efforts. What English people don't know is that English is one of the hardest languages to learn, and that children all over the world slave for years to master it. Its orthography is impenetrable, its phrasal verbs are illogical, its idioms are baffling. English people know nothing of this – indeed, they don't even know what these things are.

53.

SPEAK IN COCKNEY RHYMING SLANG

Although English people are rarely able to speak any other languages, some of them do speak Cockney rhyming slang. This originated in London's East End in the mid-nineteenth century, possibly as a way of confusing non-Cockney incomers to the district, possibly as a form of communication in the Cockney mafia.

Cockney rhyming slang is formed by replacing a word with a rhyming phrase, and then (usually) taking the first word of the new phrase to stand in for the original word. An example would be 'loaf', meaning 'head'; 'head' rhymes with 'loaf of bread', which is then abbreviated to 'loaf' (as in the common expression 'use your loaf', or 'please think carefully'). So 'feet' becomes 'plates of meat' (or just 'plates'); 'eyes' becomes 'mince pies' (or just 'minces'); and 'look' becomes 'butcher's hook' (or just 'butcher's', as in 'take a butcher's').

These are just the well-known ones: there are thousands of others. Some are based on London landmarks ('Hampstead Heath' for 'teeth', 'Chalk Farms' for 'arms') and others on popular entertainers ('Ruby Murray' for 'curry' and 'Pete Tong' for 'wrong'). Cockney rhyming slang is constantly changing. Recent coinages include 'Emma Freuds' for 'haemorrhoids' and 'Ayrton Senna' for 'tenner' (= ten pound note).

Meanwhile there is an argot known as 'Mockney', which is the accent used by members of the middle and upper classes who wish to prove they are in touch with working-class people. It was most embarrassingly deployed by Prime Minister Tony Blair, who sought to demonstrate by softening his dental plosives that he knew about life on the inner-city streets of England.

54.

RECITE 'INVICTUS'

'Invictus' – Latin for 'Unconquered' – is a poem written by WE Henley in 1875. It is one of the great expressions of English stoicism. Here it is in full:

INVICTUS

Out of the night that covers me,
Black as the pit from pole to pole,
I thank whatever gods may be
For my unconquerable soul.

In the fell clutch of circumstance
I have not winced nor cried aloud.
Under the bludgeonings of chance
My head is bloody, but unbowed.

Beyond this place of wrath and tears
Looms but the Horror of the shade,

And yet the menace of the years
Finds and shall find me unafraid.

It matters not how strait the gate,
How charged with punishments the scroll,
I am the master of my fate:
I am the captain of my soul.

Henley wrote this poem in his early twenties during a period of crisis: he was suffering from tuberculosis of the bone, and had to have one leg amputated below the knee. Despite this, and despite the continuing threat to his health, the poem expresses his unquenchable defiance of life's 'menace' and his dignity in the face of pain. Among the countless people who have been inspired by it is Nelson Mandela, who recited it to his fellow prisoners on Robben Island.

55.

READ A BOOK BY PG WODEHOUSE

PG Wodehouse wrote over ninety novels and short-story collections, as well as numerous stage-plays and musicals. His greatest characters include Bertie Wooster, the archetypal foppish Englishman; Jeeves, Bertie's 'gentleman's gentleman'; Lord Emsworth, the seigneur of Blandings Castle; Psmith, an infuriatingly emollient Old Etonian socialist; and Ukridge, an impoverished get-rich-quick merchant.

Wodehouse's particular vision of Englishness was, of course, a comic fantasy of England, one which was never 'true', and one that got progressively less 'true' as he continued writing, without alteration, into an age of nuclear weapons and digital computers. But such was its power that it continues to shape how the English (and the rest of the world) see Englishness.

Cheerful wastrels and their domineering aunts, earls and their gout-ridden butlers, adenoidal curates and their muscular bishops: these all have deep roots in the English consciousness, as if they have somehow always existed, and Wodehouse did not so much create them as lead them blinking into the light.

Wodehouse was interned as German prisoner of war in 1940-41, and later made some ill-advised radio broadcasts on German radio. This led to his vilification in the British media and his exile from England in the after-war years. In 1967 he was put forward as a possible recipient of the Companion of Honour, but was turned down: the real reason was the radio broadcasts, but the British ambassador in Washington said that the honour would 'give currency to a Bertie Wooster image of the British character which we are doing our best to eradicate.'

It was an utterly crass remark. What he meant, of course, was 'the English character'.

56.

READ A BOOK BY BARBARA CARTLAND

Another prolific and much-loved English author is Barbara Cartland. She sold over a billion romance novels, and in one year, 1983, produced 23 of them.

Here are some of the plots:

When Rena's father dies she is alone in the world, forced out of the vicarage that has been her home. (*The Cross of Love*)

When Rosina's dear friend leapt to her death after the man she loved betrayed her, she vowed vengeance. (*Love is Triumphant*)

At the ball that was to change her life, Rona Trafford danced with a mysterious Harlequin. (*Love Becomes Theirs*)

These pink-jacketed books with their virgins and heroes – despite being extremely cheesy – continue to be wildly popular throughout the world.

In an astonishing life (she lived to be 98) Barbara Cartland did much more than write. As a young woman she was a society beauty and pioneer aviator who played a leading part in the development of gliders. She campaigned for the rights of gypsies, establishing several gypsy encampments, the first of which was known as Barbaraville. She appeared regularly on television promoting her ideas on vitamins, cookery, midwifery and health foods, released an album of love songs performed by herself, and was step-grandmother to Diana, Princess of Wales (who she didn't get on with very well). In later life she dressed entirely in pink. In her 98th year one of her last acts was to launch a pink website from a pink computer.

ENGLISH ACTIVITIES

57.

SING 'JERUSALEM'

'Jerusalem' is a poem written by William Blake, and set to music by Sir Hubert Parry. Its opening words refer to the legend that Jesus visited England some time in the first century AD:

> And did those feet in ancient time
> Walk upon England's mountains green?

It ends:

> I will not cease from Mental Fight,
> Nor shall my Sword sleep in my hand:
> Till we have built Jerusalem,
> In England's green and pleasant Land.

The poem is full of phrases that have profound resonances for the English: 'dark Satanic mills' (a reference to industrialization, or to the Church, or to something else entirely), 'chariots of fire' (a biblical reference taken up in the title of the 1981 film *Chariots of Fire*), and 'green and pleasant land' (synonymous with England, though often used ironically). The song was adopted by the Suffragettes in 1917, and later associated with the Women's Institutes, who owned the copyright until the 1960s.

'Jerusalem' is heard everywhere: at sporting contests (particularly football and rugby league), at the Last Night of the Proms (see above), at wedding and funeral services, and as a soundtrack in films and television programmes. It is unique, in that despite its strong patriotic and religious content it has been taken up and claimed by every segment of English society: the extreme Left, the extreme Right, supporters of foreign wars, their opponents, environmentalists, their opponents, and so on. It is, in effect, an unofficial national anthem.

58.

SEND A NAUGHTY POSTCARD

There is only one form of handwritten postal communication that continues to thrive in England: the comic postcard. Millions are still sent annually from English seaside resorts. Most of them are rude.

The heyday of the bawdy seaside postcard was in the mid-twentieth century, when its greatest exponent was Donald McGill. He created around 12,000 designs, and today his original artwork can fetch thousands of pounds. His stock characters include huge-breasted middle-aged women, tiny henpecked husbands, drunken men lusting after promenading belles, amorous courting couples and Scotsmen wearing kilts (with the inevitable speculation about what lies beneath them.)

Early postcards of the McGill type had to be careful to avoid censorship, and so often used innuendo or suggestion, making them especially witty. In one celebrated card, two women are talking, and one says: 'Didn't she marry him after all?', and the other replies: 'No, he had a bad accident and it was broken off.' In another, a young woman is saying to a vicar: 'That was a splendid sermon about the Foolish Virgins, Vicar. I'll never be one again.'

Cards after the 1960s tended to make more obvious reference to sex, though were still influenced by the stock seaside characters. In one, a couple (henpecked husband, huge wife) are shown in bed, with the man saying to the woman: 'Do you think the doctor could do anything to help with my sex drive?' She replies: 'He can heal the sick, not raise the dead!' In another, a drunken motorist is being booked by an attractive policewoman. 'Anything you say will be taken down,' she says. 'Knickers!' he replies.

59.

BUILD SOMETHING WITH MECCANO

On a more innocent note, Meccano is a system for creating toy trains, boats, cars, cranes, bridges and other structures using small pre-fabricated strips of metal. It was invented by Frank Hornby (who went on to manufacture a highly successful series of model trains and cars) in 1901, and probably achieved its greatest popularity in the period from the 1920s to the 1950s, when Meccano sets were exported all over the world.

The typical image of the Meccano enthusiast probably comes from some time in the 1930s: he would be a schoolboy looking like 'Just William' from the stories of Richmal Crompton, in very long short trousers, wearing a school tie and a cap set slightly askew. The glory days of Meccano coincided with an era in which England was still the Workshop of the World, and English exports were big business. The era's confidence is encapsulated in a popular advertising headline of the 1920s – 'Meccano Erector Sets – Boys Today, Men Tomorrow!'

Meccano actually had a surprising influence on the development of science and technology. Scientists trying to create working prototypes of their ideas often used it. For example, Meccano was used in the construction of one of the earliest analogue computers in 1934.

Nowadays Meccano is manufactured in France and China, and the parts (increasingly of plastic) involve sophisticated electric motors, computer chips and wi-fi interfaces. These things are somewhat despised by Meccano purists, who tend to be men of a certain age. In fact, the image of the tank-topped man-who-has-never-quite-grown-up, in his attic hideout playing with Meccano or model trains, is a peculiarly English one.

60.

WALK AN ENGLISH SETTER

After your full English breakfast, perhaps while listening to the Shipping Forecast with a novel by PG Wodehouse propped up on the toast-rack, why not don your tweeds and go for a walk with your English Setter?

The English Setter was originally bred as a gun dog (the 'set' is the position the dog habitually takes when indicating the presence of a bird) but is now popular as a family pet. English Setters are related to the other setters – the Irish and the Gordon Setters – but the English will tend to be white with black or tan flecks, or, less commonly, liver or lemon flecks. English Setters are noted for their even temperament, ease of training, and gentleness. As one noted fancier of English Setters (Captain Will Judy) said: 'English Setters are gentlemen by nature. They are of the best disposition, without fear or viciousness, mild-mannered, loving and devoted every moment of their lives, and a setter's eye is one of the jewels of the entire animal kingdom.' That sounds rather as if you could wear a Setter's eye as a brooch, but he was right: the English Setter does have an eye of a rather mournfully beautiful lustre.

Walking an English Setter on a towpath or in a park will give you an excuse for a very English activity: initiating pet-mediated social interaction. The English are often incapable of talking to other English humans without the intermediary of an animal. In the early stages, the two humans involved will address their remarks only to the animals, accompanied by stroking, touching and cooing, and will graduate only later, if at all, to recognizing the presence of the other human.

61.

DRIVE A MINI

The Mini is a small car that makes, somehow, a very English statement.

It had rather unpromising origins. The Suez Crisis of 1956 had led to petrol rationing, and gas-guzzling saloons and estates were expensive to run. A young designer called Alec Issigionis (later Sir Alec) took on the challenge of designing a fuel-efficient car that would fit into a tiny box no more than 10ft long, 4ft wide and 4ft high; the only luxury of space permitted was in the side pockets of the doors, which had to be wide enough to accommodate a bottle of Gordon's gin.

The Mini was an ugly little beast, but its defiant chippiness captured patriotic sentiment and it became an icon of the Swinging '60s. Its celebrity drivers included John Lennon, George Harrison, Peter Sellers, Marianne Faithfull and Marc Bolan (Bolan in fact died when the Mini in which he was a passenger hit a tree). Later models of the Mini included the Mini Cooper, which became a highly successful rally car. The Mini's moment of greatest glory was probably the film *The Italian Job* (1969), in which Michael Caine used three Minis to stage a bullion heist, evading the Carabinieri by driving down flights of steps, through sewers and across the roofs of buildings.

What is the English statement that the Mini makes? Perhaps this: 'I'm small, I look like Harold Wilson and I have all the style of a washing machine, but I'm up for a scrap and can outpace any Italian.'

62.

RIDE ON A ROUTEMASTER

The red double-decker London bus is another motorized icon of England. Its colour chimes in well with the red postbox, the red telephone box and the St George's Cross.

There are several designs of double decker bus, but the Routemaster, with its pole at the back to grip onto, is the best-known and best-loved. The Routemaster is still the type that features on placemats, keychains, postcards and other tourist paraphernalia.

Most Routemasters were withdrawn from service in 2005, mainly because wheelchair-users couldn't board them, but it's still possible to ride one on either of two 'heritage routes' which run conveniently past many touristic hotspots, such as the Royal Albert Hall, Hyde Park Corner, Piccadilly Circus, Trafalgar Square, the Strand, the Monument and Tower Hill. Meanwhile a new, revamped Routemaster, with a conductor, a pole, and a rather extraordinary diagonal window design, came into service in 2012.

Passengers of a certain age have fond memories of attempting to grab the pole of a moving Routemaster, missing and being flung into the gutter; or worse, lying drunkenly on the floor of the platform, head sticking out into the road, skull gently bouncing on the tarmac each time the bus goes over a bump.

63.

GO TO A JUMBLE SALE

The English jumble sale is typically held in a church hall on a Saturday morning. It is organized by elderly female communicants with small moustaches. The 'jumble' they sell is junk collected from local houses by boy scouts or girl guides, and the proceeds of the sale of the junk goes towards mending the church roof (thus preventing the bells from collapsing through the belfry floor while the service is in progress).

The jumble itself is chiefly clothing, is no more than 20p per item, and is piled up in malodorous mounds at breast height. The piles contain a good salting of sequined vests, trousers with 58-inch waists, miscellaneous wigs and amorphous knitted Things. What is not clothing is designated 'bric-a-brac', and provides much of the fascination of the jumble sale. Typical bric-a-brac items will include: board games with no rules or pieces; place-mat sets of British birds; old

VHS cassettes with titles such as 'How to Cut Your Family's Hair' and 'Yorkshire Steam-Trams'; lego covered in dried jam and carpet fluff; chipped rotary cake-stands; paperbacks by Dick Francis, Alastair MacLean and Georgette Heyer; cloth flowers; worn cutlery; sachets of coffee from foreign hotels; pieces of Scalextric track; and the occasional priceless Turner sketch.

Whoever stumbles into such a paradise may consider themselves at the very heart of Englishness.

64.

GO PUNTING AT OXFORD OR CAMBRIDGE

It's surprisingly cheap to punt at Oxford or Cambridge. You can take six people out for an hour and still get change from £20. That's because (unlike taking a gondola in Venice, for example), it's a do-it-yourself activity, and you learn on the job. The result is that a good proportion of first-time punters return damp and with ruined mobile phones.

Punts are propelled from the rear with a pole (aluminium in Oxford, wood in Cambridge) which the punter pushes against the river bottom (the Isis in Oxford, the Cam in Cambridge). There is also a paddle if the punter loses the pole. This is a frequent occurrence, because the mud of the river bottom can generate a strong suction, and if the pole gets stuck, the punter can be left clinging to it like a koala on a branch. This usually ends in a wetting, because the passengers are laughing so hard they forget to help.

One popular sport for the seasoned punter is 'bridge-hopping', whereby the punter puts down his pole as the punt approaches a low bridge, and, as the punt goes under, clambers up onto the bridge, traverses it and lets himself down into the punt on the other side. This is not recommended for bridges that carry heavy traffic.

One stretch of the river at Oxford, 'Parson's Pleasure', is known as a place where the dons formerly bathed naked. The story goes that a group of bathing dons were once surprised by a puntload of ladies. The dons concealed the offending parts of their anatomy, but one covered his face. Later he explained to his colleagues: 'I can't answer for the rest of you, but I wished to cover that part of myself by which I am generally recognized.'

65.

BIKE TO HOLY COMMUNION THROUGH THE MISTS OF AN AUTUMN MORNING

George Orwell was an acute observer of Englishness, and in his 1941 essay 'England Your England' he listed a number of characteristic English things, among them 'old maids biking to Holy Communion through the mists of the autumn morning'. By 'Holy Communion' he meant specifically the Anglican version of Communion (the Eucharist) that takes place in the Church of England. By 'old maids' he meant, in 1941, any woman over thirty-five years old.

Anglicanism says a lot about England. English people feel uncomfortable with strong assertions about transcendental realities, and are generally content with a mild agnosticism. If there is an afterlife, they'll see what it's like when they get there; hopefully some form of tea will be available. They rarely attend church, except for weddings and funerals. The Church of England is the institutional expression of this vagueness. Even its priests are happy with the idea that other religions may be just as true as theirs. In 2008 the Archbishop of Canterbury, Rowan Williams, said that if parts of England were governed by Islamic *sharia* law then it wouldn't necessarily be a bad thing, and that he was sure we could all rub along together.

The Church of England is the most tolerant, placid and forgiving of all religions: it is, in its way, the best of Englishness. It is, on the whole, friendly to gay people; it ordains women; it works tirelessly in every community in the country, no matter how deprived; it owns some beautiful property; and it doesn't require that anyone make any commitment to anything.

66.

GO CHANGE-RINGING

The Church of England is a religion with a very characteristic sound. On any Sunday in any English village, town or city, it's possible to hear church bells. They usually announce a church service, but may also celebrate a wedding or other important occasion. The bells are rung not by striking with hammers (as in other parts of the world), but by pulling on ropes. The practice of ringing these bells in complicated patterns is known as change-ringing, and is found almost exclusively in England.

Change-ringing is mathematically quite complex, and the earliest published codification of its complexities is the wonderfully-named *Tintinnalogia* (1688) by Richard Duckworth and Fabian Stedman. Essentially, the more bells in a tower, the more ways there are of ringing them. A 'full peal' represents the total number of different ways a series of bells can be rung: six bells gives 720 possible permutations, seven bells 5,040, and eight bells 40,320. In fact, a full peal of eight bells has only been accomplished once in the history of bell-ringing: it was at Loughborough in 1963, and took eighteen hours. Sixteen bells would give just under 21 trillion permutations, and would take somewhat over 1,070,000 years.

Bell-ringing may be, at base, rather dry and mathematical, but the names given to the sequences of changes are not. Some of the more colourful are Tittums, Inverted Whittingtons, Jokers, Keg Meg, Weasels, Roller-coaster, Roll-ups and Exploding Hagdyke.

67.

BEAT THE BOUNDS

The 'bounds' are the limits of an English parish; and 'beating' them means walking around them, ritually beating landmarks (such as trees, important stones, etc), with sticks. Beating the Bounds is still widely carried out as part of church and community life in England. It's a way of marking the extent of the parish and reinforcing a sense of place among its inhabitants (which would have been especially important formerly, when maps were only rarely used). The procession of beaters is led by the vicar, with other members of the congregation carrying banners and flags. Hymns may be sung, scriptures chanted and commemorative markers placed. The sticks used to beat the bounds with are often of willow or birch; the English folk-song 'stripping the willow' makes reference to the beating of the bounds.

In former times it was traditional to take boys along

and whip them at strategic intervals so as to ensure they remembered where the boundaries of the parish were, and could do the same to their own children in the fullness of time. Occasionally the boys' cries might be calmed by the presentation of a small coin (or as we might term it now, 'hush-money').

Beating the Bounds is likely to have a pre-Christian origin, as with much else in English life. In fact, whenever one encounters any particularly savage or inexplicable English act, such as two scantily-clad girls fighting in heels in front of a taxi rank, it's best to nod judiciously and say under one's breath: 'Ah, yes, pre-Christian.'

68.

CELEBRATE GUY FAWKES' NIGHT

Guy Fawkes' Night, also called Bonfire Night or Fireworks Night, is an annual celebration, mainly in England, of the uncovering of a plot by Guy Fawkes and other Catholic conspirators to blow up the House of Lords on 5 November 1605. The plotters had introduced tons of gunpowder into a cellar below Parliament, and were discovered only moments before detonating it; had it gone off, it would have killed King James I, who happened to be sitting in state at the time. Guy Fawkes betrayed his fellow plotters under torture, and they were rounded up and executed.

From that very first year, bonfires were lit all over England to celebrate the King's deliverance. Effigies of Guy Fawkes (known as 'guys') were burned, often alongside effigies of the Pope and the Devil (and, much later, hate-figures such as Margaret Thatcher). Children traditionally made the 'guy' from old clothes and a mask, and the custom of begging 'a penny for the guy' on street corners was common from the eighteenth century onwards. (In the twenty-first century the custom has largely died out, with children now seemingly disdainful of collecting pennies.) Bonfire Night, as it is more commonly called, has now lost its anti-Catholic associations and is more of a family celebration, with firework parties in private gardens and public parks. Various parts of the country have their own Guy Fawkes Night traditions, such as that of Ottery St Mary, Devon, where barrels of flaming tar are carried through the streets.

Guy Fawkes is sometimes said to be 'the only man ever to have entered Parliament with honest intentions'.

69.

SUPPORT A FRINGE PARTY

Fringe political parties are highly esteemed in England, a country that values humour and does not always take its politicians very seriously.

Fringe parties are most prominent at by-elections (held for example due to the retirement in disgrace of a Member of Parliament), which receive disproportionate media attention and give fringe parties a chance to shine.

The best known of the English fringe parties is the Monster Raving Loony Party, founded in the 1980s by David 'Screaming Lord' Sutch. Among the better-known policies of the Monster Raving Loony Party are: 'All politicians should paint themselves permanently from head to toe in the colour of the party they represent', and 'Anyone allowing their hyena to poop on the pavement should shovel it away immediately, as this is no laughing matter.' Other

English fringe parties have included the I Want to Drop a Blancmange Down Terry Wogan's Y-Fronts Party, the Fancy Dress Party, the Church of the Militant Elvis Party, the None of the Above Party and the Teddy Bear Alliance. A characteristic English entertainment is watching television coverage of an election and relishing the point where the returning officer is forced to read out the names of these silly parties.

One of the most famous fringe parties of recent years was the cunning Literal Democrat Party, which stood in the European elections of 1994. Its close similarity in name with the mainstream Liberal Democrat Party deceived 10,203 voters into supporting it, and caused the real Liberal Democrats to lose to the Conservatives.

70.

ATTEND A SWAN UPPING

Swans were formerly highly prized for their meat, and the swans on the River Thames in London are still the property of the Queen. Swan Upping is a ceremony performed every year in July. Fleets of boats belonging to two ancient trade guilds, the Vintners and the Dyers, and a third fleet belonging to the Queen, carry out a survey of the swans on the river, and mark the beaks of the cygnets with sharp knives. The patterns on the beaks show that they belong to either the Vintners, Dyers or Queen's Swan Uppers. The Dyers give their swans one nick on the side of the beak, the Vintners two nicks, one on each side, and the Queen's swans are left unmarked. The custom of giving two nicks is reflected in the pub name 'The Swan with Two Necks', 'neck' being a corruption of 'nick'. (Pubs with this name are found all over England.) 'The 'Upping' in 'Swan Upping' probably refers to the 'taking up' of the swans from the river in order to mark them.

Swan Upping is a highly colourful spectacle and takes place over five days, with a timetable published well in advance, so it is easy to view an Upping at a number of locations along the Thames. The boats all fly ornate flags featuring pictures of swans and the Swan Uppers wear traditional costumes.

Very few people can be found who have tried swan meat, because the swan is a protected species of bird, but those who have are often not impressed. Swans exist on a diet of weed, snails, small fish, tadpoles and insects, and the resulting flavour is apparently that of a fishy, muddy turkey.

71.

DO THE FURRY DANCE

The Furry Dance is another English custom that stretches back in time almost to prehistory. As with many other English traditions, the Furry Dance has an air almost of melancholy: one imagines the generations who have taken part in the dance and whose bones have been absorbed into the land.

The Furry dance is not notably furry. 'Furry' probably derives from 'feur', a Celtic word meaning 'festival'. It takes place annually in May at Helston, in Cornwall, and draws visitors from around the world. The dancers are, first, paired men and women, dancing to a tune known as the 'Floral Dance' (made famous by the Brighouse and Rastrick brass band); and, secondly, the children of the schools around Helston, wearing flowers in their hair or sporting coloured ties.

Later on in the day there is a performance of the 'Hal-an-Tow', a play notable for its anti-Spanish propaganda. These references probably date from the Anglo-Spanish war of 1585-1604, during which a Spanish fleet landed in Cornwall and pillaged its coastal towns. The Spaniards were ultimately sent packing, as the 'Hal-an-Tow' makes clear:

What happened to the Spaniards
Who made so great a boast O?
It's they shall eat the feathered goose
And we shall eat the roast O!

ENGLISH SPORTS

72.

PLAY POOHSTICKS

Poohsticks is a game that derives from the children's book *The House at Pooh Corner* by AA Milne. In the book, Winnie-the-Pooh says that he has invented a game in which the players throw sticks from a bridge into a stream, then wait for them to emerge on the other side of the bridge; the first stick to emerge is the winner.

Because the game is largely played by children or the mentally undeveloped, there is often an argument about whose stick it is that has emerged first, because the players have not taken any care to distinguish their sticks from one another. Sticks also commonly get stuck under the bridge or are dropped in at the wrong side of the bridge and float away in the wrong direction, usually to howls.

Before the game featured in the Winnie-the-Pooh stories, it was played in real life by AA Milne and his son Christopher Robin, and the bridge on which it was first played can still be seen in Ashdown Forest, near Upper Hartfield, East Sussex. The bridge receives thousands of visitors a year from all over the world, who have been responsible for denuding nearby trees of their branches. Visitors are now politely requested to bring their own sticks.

A note on class: Poohsticks is enjoyed by middle-class and upper-class English people, and not by working-class people or those living in the North.

73.

PLAY CROQUET

Croquet sounds as if it ought to be French, but it's English. It *may* have been imported from France into England in the mid-17th century, but even if so, croquet is now only rarely played in France, and France is not a member country of the World Croquet Federation (which includes England, Scotland, South Africa, Australia, New Zealand, Canada, Egypt, Italy, Japan, Ireland and the USA).

Croquet involves hitting coloured balls through hoops and cheating. It is one of those games that in England is infected by class sensitivity. Regardless of who actually plays it – and it is played by a wide variety of people – it is thought of as an upper-middle-class or upper-class game. This is possibly because of its association with the monarchy in days gone by, or perhaps because of its image as a sedate game played by ladies in elaborate gowns in films by Merchant and Ivory; or perhaps because of its appearance in sophisticated writings such as *Alice's Adventures in Wonderland*, where Alice joins in a croquet match using flamingos for mallets.

Croquet was at the centre of a very English scandal in 2006, when the Deputy Prime Minister, the impeccably working-class (and Northern) John Prescott, was discovered playing croquet at his mansion at Dorneywood at a time when he was supposed to be running the country. Prescott was attacked from all quarters, not so much because he didn't deserve a little recreation, but because an oik from Hull shouldn't have been messing around with mallets unless he was driving in a fence-post. Of course no one could be found who would actually *say* this.

74.

PLAY CRICKET

The English historian George Macaulay Trevelyan said in his *English Social History*: 'If the French noblesse had been capable of playing cricket with their peasants, their chateaux would never have been burnt.'

This is a large claim, and needs some examination.

Cricket began in the 16th century as a game played on farms. In the 17th century it spread rapidly throughout the south of England, particularly in the counties around London. By the 18th century, cricket was big business. The leisured aristocracy had taken it up, along with horse racing and pugilism, chiefly as a vehicle for betting: fabulous sums were wagered on single games, which naturally led to the earliest match fixing. It was also a sport in which the gentry and commoners mixed on equal terms. Landowners were keen to get the best players for their teams, and would often employ men as butlers or gardeners just to get them as players (thus leading to early transfer deals and the rise of professionalism in sports). On the field, aristocrat and peasant mixed. In England in the 18th century it was possible for a drayman to dismiss a duke for a duck. In France at the same time this would have been unthinkable.

Cricket is widely supposed to have inculcated many of the English virtues. 'Not guillotining one another' is possibly one of the least recognized.

75.

PLAY CONKERS

Conkers is a traditional English game played with the shiny brown seeds ('conkers') of horse chestnut trees. They are threaded on lengths of string, and players strike their conkers against one another until one of them breaks. The game was first recorded in 1848, but is almost certainly of greater antiquity.

Modern play has become somewhat cramped by health and safety concerns. In 2008 it was widely reported that the Health and Safety Executive, a government agency, had stipulated that plastic goggles should be used while playing conkers in order to obviate the danger of nut-shards entering the players' eyes. This diktat was treated with contempt as an example of 'political correctness gone mad' (a phrase that the English utter at least three times daily), though in fact the story was later proved to be false, and indeed the Executive later sponsored a conker game to demonstrate how relaxed and friendly and reasonable they were, an event that was sadly under-reported.

Undeterred, the World Conker Championship, held annually at Ashton in Northamptonshire, continues to attract conker-athletes from all over the world. To prevent cheating, such as the pre-hardening of conkers in vinegar, the Ashton Conker Club supplies all conkers and strings. Rules include the following:

> Each player takes three alternate strikes at the opponent's conker. If these six strikes last for more than five minutes then play will halt and the 5-minute rule will come into effect. Each player will be allowed up to nine further strikes at their opponent's nut, again alternating three strikes each. If neither conker has been smashed at the end of the nine strikes then the player who strikes the nut the most times during this period will be judged the winner.

76.

GO ON A FUN RUN

'Fun' and 'run' rhyme, which has spawned an activity that involves thousands of English people a year. A fun run is not, however, much fun. It involves jogging over a set distance, often wearing a silly costume, for the purpose of raising money for charity, usually by people who are not physically very fit. Each fun runner must find sponsors, which means annoying friends and work colleagues for weeks beforehand.

The fun run is a trade-off. The sponsors are revenged on the runner because the runner undertakes to run the course dressed in a nappy, chicken costume or diving suit. Or perhaps the runner is physically challenged in some way and can locomote only with very great pain and difficulty, making them unable to complete the course in under three weeks, rendering them an English hero (since 'playing the game' is more important than winning).

Some of the people who go on fun runs do seem to be having a genuinely good time, especially when collapsing at the tape. But it is hard to avoid the conclusion that there are no fun driving tests because 'driving test' does not rhyme with 'fun', there are no fun wars because 'war' does not rhyme with 'fun', and there are no fun diseases because 'disease' does not rhyme with 'fun'.

77.

GO EXTREME IRONING

Extreme ironing may be defined as a quest for thrills while simultaneously achieving a perfect crease. Participants go skydiving, potholing, bungee-jumping or skiing, only with an ironing board and iron. Occasionally they iron while standing on top of monuments or at busy traffic intersections. There is an annual world championship sponsored by the iron manufacturer Rowenta, and winners have included a team who ironed while negotiating the Wolfberg Cracks in the Cederberg Mountains of South Africa.

Extreme ironing started in Leicestershire, England, in 1997, when a worker at a knitwear factory, Phil Shaw (known as 'Steam'), wanted to go rock-climbing but also needed to do the ironing, and decided to unite the two activities. It quickly became a sport with an international dimension (England seems to like exporting its sports), and there are now extreme ironing athletes in Germany, Austria, New Zealand, Australia, Croatia and South Africa. Ironing underwater is a popular variant on the theme, and in 2008 in Gloucestershire, 86 divers managed to iron underwater at the same time. The irons were not electric irons, or if they were, they were not plugged in.

The official guidance of the Extreme Ironing Board notes: 'Pay attention to weather conditions, and never extreme iron on your own. The nature of some extreme iron sessions is such that it would be foolhardy to attempt them without backup.'

78.

EAT NETTLES

The Bottle Inn at Marshwood, Dorset, is the venue for the World Stinging Nettle Eating Championships, held annually in June.

The tradition dates to 1986, when two farmers had an argument about who had the longest stinging nettles on his land. One, Alex Williams, tried to settle the argument by bringing in a monster 15ft-long stinging nettle, saying he would eat it if anyone could find a longer nettle; subsequently a longer nettle was produced, and Mr Williams was forced to keep his word.

The rules are simple: competitors are supplied with stinging nettles in two-foot lengths (to make judging easier) and must strip the leaves off them and eat them raw as quickly as possible. They are allowed to anaesthetize their tongues with beer. Hundreds of people spectate, though the number of contestants is kept to sixty-five.

Stinging nettles produce their 'sting' with thousands of tiny hypodermic needles that discharge boric acid. On contact, the needles break and produce a painful skin rash. The best way to eat nettles, therefore, is to ball the leaves up into little packages and try to swallow them without too much chewing. Nevertheless, mouth-to-nettle contact can lead to facial paralysis, and the organizers look out for so-called 'green-bearding', in which the mouth muscles become so slack that viridian drool runs down the chin forming a goatee: the competitor is then advised to quit.

Both the original farmers are now dead.

79.

GO TOE-WRESTLING

Toe-wrestling is like thumb-wrestling, only with feet. The two competitors ceremonially take off their shoes and socks, then lock toes on the 'Toedium'. At the chant of 'One, two, three, four, I declare toetal war', each tries to force their opponent's toe down to touch one edge of the 'Toesrack' (a move known as 'toe down'). The rules state: 'A player may, if the agony becomes too great, surrender by calling out the words 'toe much': the winning player should then immediately release their toe hold.' The rules additionally state: 'Each match is the best of three legs.'

Toe-wrestling began in Wetton, Derbyshire, in the 1970s. The sport's founder was one George Burgess, whose idea was to create an event that even an English team could win. The first world champion was unfortunately a Canadian who happened to be visiting Wetton on the day. The current title holder is Alan 'Nasty' Nash, who has broken his toes nine times in pursuit of international glory. His competitors include Paul Beech, aka the Toeminator, and the Itoelion Stallion from Milan.

The world's press regularly attend the world championships in June, at the Bentley Brook Inn near Ashbourne, Derbyshire, and beam images around the world. Japan has been a particularly enthusiastic consumer of the sport, which is not surprising, given its similarity to sumo wrestling, only without the dignity and skill.

80.

GO CHEESE-ROLLING

With a cry of 'One to be ready! Two to be steady! Three to prepare! And four to be off!' a 8-pound Double Gloucester cheese is set rolling down Cooper's Hill in Gloucestershire on the last Monday of May. Screaming villagers run pell-mell after the cheese down the 1:2 incline, many falling over and suffering sprains and broken bones. The first to get to the bottom of the hill wins the cheese. Many others win an ambulance.

As with most of England's traditions, the exact antiquity of cheese-rolling is uncertain. It may date back thousands of years and derive from fertility rituals, perhaps of the Saxons, perhaps of the Romans, perhaps of the Phoenicians. It has certainly been recorded for over two hundred years; during this time it has only been interrupted once, by the Second World War, when all foodstuffs were strictly rationed.

During this time, instead of a real cheese, a wooden one was used, containing a small piece of symbolic cheese in a special niche.

In recent years the cheese-rolling has attracted spectators from all over the world, and the recently-levied spectator's fee of £20 has led to death threats against the organizers, who, already under threat of death by broken neck, have failed to let it bother them.

81.

GO BOTTLE-KICKING

Bottle-kicking is an ancient English custom that does not involve bottles or, particularly, kicking. It takes place each year on Easter Monday between the people of the village of Hallaton, Leicestershire, and the residents of nearby Medbourne. Only Hallaton people can be members of the Hallaton team, though Medbourne will accept anyone. Bottle-kicking is a bit like rugby, only played over a wider area and with gallon kegs of beer rather than balls; the object is to get the kegs of beer to a touchline in either village.

The action kicks off in Hallaton after a ceremony involving the distribution of a hare pie. The story goes that at some time in the distant past, two Hallaton women were wending their way across the fields when they were charged by a bull. At the last moment, when it seemed that a goring was inevitable, a hare ran in front of the bull and distracted it. The women escaped, and in gratitude for their deliverance they paid for a hare pie and beer to be distributed annually to the poor. (If they were so grateful to the hare, it would surely have made more sense to give up eating hares.) After the pie is eaten, the beer phase begins, which is where the bottle-kicking comes in.

The tradition is recorded as far back as the eighteenth century, but may be of much greater antiquity, possibly even pre-Christian antiquity. One Hallaton vicar did try to ban the event in 1790, but changed his mind when the following words were found scrawled on his wall: 'No pie, no parson.'

82.

RUN IN A PANCAKE RACE

Olney, in Buckinghamshire, is the venue for this English tradition held annually on Shrove Tuesday (the Tuesday immediately before Lent, traditionally a time for games and jests). The pancake race is open to women over 18 years who have lived in the village for more than six months. Racers are expected to wear the traditional garb of the housewife (dress, apron, headscarf) and carry a frying pan and pancake. They must toss the pancake at least once at the start of the race, and once at the end of the race. The course itself is over a 415-yard distance, from the market to the parish church.

Pancake racing at Olney is of very great antiquity: the first run was in 1445. Tradition has it that the first racer was a woman who was late for the shriving service (when sins are forgiven in preparation for Lent). Running from her house to the church, desperate to be shriven, she forgot that she was still wearing her apron and carrying a frying pan.

Pancake racing has not yet been professionalized, and so the only prize is a kiss from the verger.

83.

GO GURNING

Held annually in mid-September, the Egremont Crab Fair dates back to the 13th century. In this case a 'crab' is not a crustacean, but an apple. The Fair features a day of events, the highlight of which, capturing the most media attention, is the World Gurning Championships.

To 'gurn' is to contort the face into strange and unlovely shapes. The contestant who can look most like they are turning their heads inside out, sticking out the lower jaw out to engulf most of the rest of the face or protruding the tongue so as to caress the earlobe, wins. There is a male, a female and a junior category; the first female entrant was Mrs Mabel Braddock in 1966. Gurning takes place on a stage, and the winner is the contestant who provokes the loudest shrieks. The gurner is required to make their gurn through a horse's braffin, or collar.

Although it is a live event, anyone can visit the Egremont Gurning website and upload a photo of themselves gurning, and may win the title of Gurner of the Month and a prize of a 'Cumbrian facepack': some Lake District mud and two slices of rancid cucumber.

ENGLISH PLACES

84.

VISIT PARLIAMENT

Many visitors to England – and many English people themselves – are unaware that it's possible to visit Parliament. On Saturdays throughout the year, and six days a week in the Summer, visitors can go on a guided tour that takes in the House of Commons, the House of Lords, the Queen's Robing Room, the Royal Gallery and Westminster Hall. Foreign visitors and UK residents may sit in the public gallery and watch debates in the House of Commons and House of Lords, and may even attend Prime Minister's Questions (the highlight of the parliamentary week).

Most of the actual buildings (Big Ben, the House of Commons, etc.) were built comparatively recently, after a disastrous fire in the 19th century, but there are still some survivals from earlier eras, notably Westminster Hall, which was begun in 1097 by the son of William the Conqueror.

Tickets for the standard tour are easy to get by queuing at the ticket office next to the Jewel Tower opposite the Houses of Parliament. Alternatively, tickets can be booked online. Tours in French, German, Italian and Spanish are available. For UK residents the news is even better: the tours are free if booked through a Member of Parliament, and it's possible to climb Big Ben, also for free, if booked in advance.

One note of clarification: the parliament at Westminster is not the English parliament but the United Kingdom parliament. England doesn't have its own parliament.

85.

GO TO GREENWICH

Because it's south of the River Thames, many people don't take the opportunity of visiting Greenwich, but it's one of the loveliest and most fascinating spots in London.

The first thing to do at Greenwich is to go to the Observatory and see the famous meridian, the line that forms the zero degree longitude circle running from pole to pole, and jump from one side to the other of it. This is a deeply childish but deeply satisfying thing to do.

The second thing to do is to visit the Planetarium, which takes visitors on a journey into the wonders of the universe in glorious HD. Since the closing of the Planetarium in Marylebone Road, it's actually London's only planetarium.

The third thing to do is to visit the Cutty Sark, a restored racing tea clipper. Alongside is the Gypsy

Moth IV, the vessel in which an Englishman made the first true single-handed circumnavigation of the world.

The fourth thing to do is to visit the National Maritime Museum, the world's largest museum of its type, encompassing the entirety of England's seafaring past, where you can see the uniform Nelson was wearing when he was shot.

Lastly you can sit on Greenwich Hill, and see, over the stretches of rolling green, the best view of London: the 17th-century Queen's House, Greenwich University, the Thames gliding along in all its majesty, the Isle of Dogs, and Canary Wharf jutting up in the middle distance.

86.

VISIT AN AONB

Only around 20% of the land of England is inhabited by people. The remaining 80% is empty.

Well, empty: it's actually farmland or woodland. But many parts of this land are so distinctively lovely that they are protected by law. These places are known as Areas of Outstanding Natural Beauty (AONBs) and there are 33 of them in England.

Among the most beautiful AONBs are: the Chiltern Hills, the Cotswolds, Dedham Vale, the Forest of Bowland, the Kentish High Weald, the Isles of Scilly, the Lincolnshire Wolds, the Malvern Hills, the Norfolk Coast, the North Wessex Downs, the Quantock Hills, the Solway Coast and the Tamar Valley. These are all open to visitors and have well-maintained trails. Sometimes these AONBs range over quite large areas (for example the Cotswolds or the North Pennines) and may encompass numerous villages and even towns. Some have world heritage status. The North Wessex Downs, for example, takes in the stone circle at Avebury, various Roman remains, and the White Horse of Uffington.

AONBs are a bulwark against urban expansion in England and most English people would agree that they should be cherished. However, most English people never see an AONB, and know about them only by hearsay, because, despite the more difficult financial climate, they still prefer to take a holiday abroad. They are thus more familiar with Goa or Sharm el-Sheik than the Pennines or the Quantocks. Foreign visitors to England's AONBs are more likely to encounter fellow nationals there than anywhere else bar Madame Tussaud's.

87.

VISIT ANNE HATHAWAY'S COTTAGE

Anne Hathaway was Shakespeare's wife. They married in 1582 when he was 18 and she 27. The disparity in their ages, and the fact that she was three months' pregnant at the time, has led to speculation that it was a shotgun wedding.

What sort of a person was Anne? In the absence of much evidence, tradition has been unkind. Shakespeare spent his career in London, leaving Anne alone to look after their three children. Some have assumed that it was a loveless marriage, and that Shakespeare got away from this sexually predatory older woman as soon as it was feasible.

But a visit to Anne Hathaway's Cottage in Shottery, near to Stratford-upon-Avon, makes one thing clear. Anne was wealthy. Her 'cottage' – her familial home before she married – was not a cottage at all, but a highly desirable, well-appointed thatched 12-room farmhouse, set in over ninety acres of land. Shakespeare's family, in contrast, were poor. A few sums make an alternative scenario possible: Anne was a reluctant bride and Shakespeare a cunning impregnator. If anyone did better out of the arrangement, it was William.

Among the furniture on show at the cottage is the Hathaway Bed, which, according to the curators, is the 'second-best bed' that Shakespeare bequeathed to Anne in his will. Does this bequest show how little he loved her? Not necessarily. A 'best bed' would have been reserved for the sole use of guests, and so a 'second-best bed' was the marital bed. It is likely that in this bed the love between Anne and William was consummated. If so, it was the most romantic bequest possible.

88.

VISIT HADRIAN'S WALL

Hadrian's Wall is a 73-mile long Roman wall built in around AD120 by decree of the Emperor Hadrian. It runs just to the south of the current border between Scotland and England, and is a UNESCO World Heritage site.

It's probably not true to say that the wall was built to protect the Romans from marauding Scottish tribes. Scotland was actually quite thinly populated at the time, and the Romans were at the height of their imperial power. It might have been simply that the Romans didn't feel there was much in Scotland worth having, and decided to mark the spot where the Empire ended. Alternatively it could have been built so as to control traffic over the border and levy taxes. No-one is quite sure.

If you visit Hadrian's Wall today you'll find much of it well preserved, especially the central section. As well as the wall itself, parts of which stand around ten feet high, there are the remains of forts, ditches, banks and watchtowers. There is free access to the wall along its length, though visitors are asked not to walk on the wall for fear of erosion.

Another Roman wall, the Antonine Wall, was built some 75 miles to the north of Hadrian's wall. The Antonine Wall is in Scotland proper and traverses the country from east to west. It was made mainly of turf, and little of it has survived. It rains quite a lot in Scotland, and mud is not the best building material.

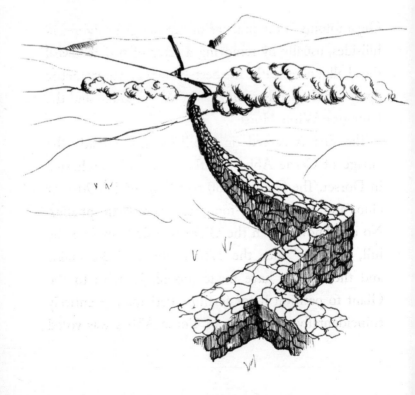

89.

VISIT THE CERNE ABBAS GIANT AND THE UFFINGTON WHITE HORSE

Gigantotomy is the practice of carving giant figures in hillsides, usually by removing a layer of turf to reveal the chalk underneath. The best-known gigantotometric figures in England are the Cerne Abbas Giant and the Uffington White Horse.

The first is carved on a hillside just outside the village of Cerne Abbas, to the north of Dorchester, in Dorset. The Giant is 180 feet long, with a 90-foot club, and sports a 20-foot gigantotometric phallus. No one knows when the Giant was first cut into the hill, but ever since the 17th century, village maids and their lovers have made moonlight trips to the Giant to petition it for fertility. Perhaps not entirely coincidentally, the village of Cerne Abbas was voted 'most desirable village in England' by the estate agents Savills in 2008.

The 374-foot Uffington White Horse is of greater antiquity than the Giant: it may be 3,000 years old. It can be found on a hillside near the parish of Uffington in Oxfordshire. With its sleek lines, low body, whiskers and absence of a mane, it looks more like a cat than a horse; but whichever animal it is, it was probably some sort of tribal symbol for its gigantotomers.

The National Trust owns both figures, and both may be viewed from the ground at close quarters for whatever purposes the visitor has in mind.

90.

VISIT STONEHENGE

Stonehenge is probably the most famous prehistoric site in the world. It is located near Salisbury, Wiltshire.

Stonehenge consists of a circle of massive stones within a series of earthworks. The date of the stones is uncertain, but the best current guess is that they are around 4,500 years old. Remarkably, some of the stones were transported to the site from North Pembrokeshire in Wales, 140 miles away.

The purpose of Stonehenge is a matter of debate. Some have said it was a type of observatory, enabling its builders to predict and celebrate astronomical events such as solstices and eclipses; others have said it was a centre of healing; yet others have said it was a cultic place enabling people to make a symbolic journey from the land of the living to the land of the dead. There are certainly some strange burials here. One skeleton, dating to 1550 BC, is of a boy whose DNA shows he must have grown up near the Mediterranean; another, the so-called 'Amesbury archer', must have originated from the Alpine regions of Germany. Whatever the true function of Stonehenge, it was clearly a place of Europe-wide significance.

Visitors are not allowed to touch the stones, and must view them from a nearby path. Exception is made for neo-pagan groups, who are allowed to approach the stones at certain times of the year and perform ceremonies, trying not to be distracted by the roar of the A303 and A344 passing nearby.

91.

CLIMB SCAFELL PIKE

England is not notably mountainous: the highest mountains are in the north of the country, and include the Cheviot Hills, the Pennines, the Yorkshire Dales, the Peak District, the Lake District, the Forest of Bowland and the North York Moors. The highest mountain in England is Scafell Pike in the Lake District, which rises to 3,209 ft (978m). Rather confusingly, the second highest mountain in England is called Sca Fell. This is immediately next door to Scafell Pike, and rises to 3,162 ft (964m), a mere 47ft lower. From some angles, Sca Fell looks higher than Scafell Pike.

Scafell Pike is the highest of the so-called Wainwrights. These are named after Alfred Wainwright, a Lake District walker, who wrote and illustrated a famous guide to the 214 peaks of the district. Climbing the Wainwrights is known as 'Wainwright-bagging', and the youngest person to have bagged them all is a five-year old boy, Sail Chapman, who completed his 214th in 2009. When interviewed on his achievement he said: 'My favourite thing about it is the sandwiches.'

ENGLISH FOOD
AND DRINK

92.

HAVE A NICE CUP OF TEA

'When I look through my own recipe for the perfect cup of tea, I find no fewer than eleven outstanding points,' says George Orwell with characteristic mock-pedantry in his classic essay 'A Nice Cup of Tea'. Among them are the following:

always make tea in a china or earthenware teapot;
always warm the teapot first;
always put the milk in last;
don't drink tea with sugar.

He doesn't mention teabags (presumably they were not in common use in 1946, when the essay was written).

England is a nation of dedicated tea-drinkers. The English get through 125,000 tonnes of black tea (sometimes called Indian tea) per year. Tea punctuates and lubricates every English social interaction. The tea break is enshrined in the rights of English employees, and any employer who seeks to prune the tea break, or restrict the biscuits associated with it, is courting strike action. Tea also has a class significance. The stronger and sweeter the tea, the likelier it is that a lower-class person will be drinking it. In fact strong, sweet tea (such as PG Tips or Typhoo) is also known as 'builders' tea', as opposed to any of the rarefied teas that are available in specialist tea shops and drunk by the middle classes (Orange Pekoe, Earl Grey, Formosa Oolong). 'Builders' tea' is expected to be served in a thick mug (not a cup), and with five sugars, so that the resulting leathery brew is 'strong enough to stand a spoon up in'.

Confusingly, 'tea' is also the name of a meal (see the next section).

93.

HAVE A NICE TEA

Tea, the drink, is so important in England that it stands in for the name of several meals. These meals are all slightly different, and are eaten at slightly different times, according to where you live in the country and what social class you belong to.

'Afternoon tea' is perhaps best known. It is 'taken' some time between three and five o'clock, and consists of tea (from a china teapot), accompanied by cake and small sandwiches (most famously cucumber sandwiches with the crusts cut off). Billowing white dresses, straw hats and a summer's day, with swans if available, are useful accessories. However, perhaps disappointingly for foreign visitors, 'afternoon tea' of this type is now scarcely ever eaten in England. The only place it is regularly served is in hotels ('tea at the Ritz').

A 'cream tea' is rather different, and consists of

cream pastries (such as scones) and tea; this can be eaten at any time of the day and is a speciality of the south-west of England.

'Tea', sometimes known as 'high tea', is an early evening meal. In the North of England in particular, this 'tea' is the main evening meal; so if someone from Barnsley invites you home for tea, expect to be fed well.

In fact, what an English person calls their evening meal is a fairly reliable indicator of class: if 'tea', they are working-class, if 'dinner', they are middle, and if 'supper', they are upper-middle or upper. However, just to confuse the picture further, the Northern working class call their midday meal 'dinner', and in some Northern working-class speech 'supper' is the name for the evening meal.

94.

EAT A FULL ENGLISH

A 'Full English' is a traditional English breakfast, also known as a fry-up, a Full Monty or a Full English Heart Attack. Its constituents vary from place to place, but stypically include bacon, eggs, fried bread, sausages, tomato, baked beans and mushrooms, all fried together and served in their own fat. The Full English can be found in its finest flowering in the traditional English greasy spoon café, where not merely the spoons but also the furniture, walls and staff have a pearly-yellow patina.

Noel Coward said that for an Englishman to eat well he need only partake of breakfast three times a day; and there are places where this advice has been taken to heart, such as southern Spain and Portugal, where tourists from Birmingham are able to scoff bacon and eggs at midnight while watching Sky and drinking Kronenbourg.

Such is the grip that this meal has on the English imagination that 'Full Englishes' are sold in tins in English grocery shops, which must surely represent the nadir of English culinary competence.

The biggest Full English in the world is served by Mario's Cafe Bar in West Houghton, near Bolton. It consists of ten rashers of bacon, ten eggs, ten sausages, ten slices of toast, as well as black pudding, baked beans, tomatoes and mushrooms, and it comes to 5,000 calories, or twice the recommended daily amount for an adult male. Anyone who can finish it off gets the meal free of charge.

95.

EAT FISH AND CHIPS

The foreign visitor who wishes to try English food is most often pointed toward fish and chips. The visitor will have heard of fish and chips before ever arriving in England, and generally can't wait to sample them, as the only contribution England has ever made to world cuisine.

Naturally the visitor is not so foolish as to expect much of the chips. 'Chips' are merely fried potatoes. The sorcery of fish and chips – a dish that somehow substitutes for gastronomy in England – must inhere in the fish. If England, a great nation, is famous for this fish, surely it must be an outstanding type of fish. It must contain all the virtues that other nations distribute among a wide range of dishes. The visitor's anticipation will be all the keener if someone tells them that this fish, this special fish, is the only thing to have survived the Reformation. How else to explain the queues that form outside fish and chip shops every Friday, the day when the Catholic church formerly proscribed all meat?

Watch the visitor as they examine this fish before eating it. They pick at it, turning it over as if they expect to find something beneath it. It is a piece of battered fish. It seems to be leaking oil in a rather disgusting way that is surely not intentional. Is this the 'fish' of fish and chips, the culinary acme of a nation?

Oh God.

96.

EAT PIE, MASH AND LIQUOR

Another traditional English dish is pie and mash, from London's East End.

The pie was traditionally made with eels, which formerly swarmed in large numbers in the River Thames. Now the eels have largely died out, and the pie is more likely to be filled with minced beef. The mash is nothing more than mashed potato. What makes pie and mash special is the sauce associated with it, known as the 'liquor'. This is traditionally made from the water that the eels have been boiled in, and is flavoured and coloured with parsley, giving it a green colour.

There are still a few pie and mash shops in London, some of them furnished in a traditional white tile as they would have been in Victorian times. Some pie and mash shops also sell jellied eels, another traditional East End dish: these are essentially eels that have been chopped into segments, boiled and then allowed to cool and set in their own juice, forming a jelly (sometimes helped along with the addition of gelatine).

Londoners formerly relied greatly on food from the Thames and its estuary, and a further staple was oysters, which were not, as now, an expensive luxury, but plentiful and cheap. They were so common, in fact, that beef pies were sometimes bulked up with bivalves to reduce costs. If oysters are an aphrodisiac, Victorian London was the sexiest place in the world.

97.

EAT A REAL CORNISH PASTY MADE IN CORNWALL

Another type of pie is the Cornish Pasty, which also has an English working-class connection: it is associated particularly with the miners of the Cornish tin industry, who would take a pasty down the mine as a cheap, portable snack. There are many traditions concerning pasties and mining. One held that a small portion of the pasty should be left to appease the spirits of the mine, known as 'knockers' (because they would make a knocking noise to alert miners to a pit collapse).

Cornish pasties now have Protected Geographical Indication status, which means that only pasties made in Cornwall can call themselves Cornish pasties (though the ingredients don't have to come from Cornwall, and the pasties can be made in Cornwall and baked elsewhere). Cornish pasties have a 'D' shape and are crimped on the rounded side, rather than on top. The filling should include no less than 12.5% beef, plus swede, potato and onion, with a peppery seasoning. Pasties are generally glazed with milk or egg to achieve a golden colour, and the pastry should be robust enough to resist cracking if dropped down a tin mine.

Pasties have a history stretching back to the 12th century, when they can be found mentioned in Arthurian romances. They were also eaten by Samuel Pepys, who recorded in his diary for Thursday 1 August 1667: 'At noon my wife and I dined at Sir W. Pen's, only with Mrs. Turner and her husband, on a damned venison pasty, that stunk like a devil.'

98.

STOP AT A ST GEORGE'S CROSS BURGER STAND

The St George's Cross, a red cross on a white background, is the flag of England. It appears within the British flag (also called the Union flag or Union Jack) as the main upright red cross: the diagonal portions of the British flag are supplied by the flags of Scotland and Ireland.

The St George's Cross is seen most commonly in the context of sporting competitions such as football or rugby. Outside these occasions, the St George's Cross is not flown very often in England; certainly not as often as the Stars and Stripes is in the USA or the tricolore is in France. Many English people hesitate to display this symbol of their nationality, in case it is seen as an assertion of supremacy over other nations – Scotland, Ireland, Wales, the countries of the British

Empire – or is misinterpreted as outright nationalistic racism. The St George's Cross, unfortunately, is tainted.

This makes the appearance of the St George's Cross, flying proudly and prominently over burger stands on main roads, an interesting phenomenon. Burger stands – little vans that sell burgers, hot dogs and tea in lay-bys – seem to fly the flag as a means of identification, as if the cross meant, not 'We support England' but 'Buy burger here', or, more frankly, 'Stop here if you are an unreconstructed fat racist.' The burgers are always made of the secondary or tertiary parts of a cow, the tea is always weak, there is always oil floating on top of it, and the patron is always Caucasian.

99.

SAVOUR AN ENGLISH APPLE

Sometimes the simplest pleasures are the best. What could be more satisfying than biting deeply and voluptuously into the succulent, encarmined flesh of a freshly-picked apple, and then, unable to resist, devouring it to the stalk, pips and all?

England offers unrivalled opportunities for this activity. The English apple season starts in August, when thousands of varieties make their appearance. They all have wonderful names: Bloody Ploughman, Pig's Snout, D'Arcy Spice, Foxwhelps, Hoary Morning, Howgate Wonder, Laxton's Fortune, Pendragon, Polly Whitehair, Ashmead's Kernel, Winter Banana and Wisley Crab.

The environmental group Common Ground has estimated that there are 3,000 varieties of English apple. In 1990 the group instituted Apple Day in Covent Garden, London, to celebrate this extraordinary and versatile fruit. Apple Day has since spread around the world.

Science suggests that an apple every eight hours can keep three doctors away. Apples prevent the development of dementia, prostate cancer, lung cancer and colon cancer, as well as helping with weight control (at around 60 calories each they are a great snack) and heart disease. Researchers in Hong Kong have found that fruit flies fed on apples lived 10% longer than fruit flies fed on a normal diet. Though, since these were fruit flies, you'd expect them to do well on apples.

100.

DRINK TRADITIONAL CIDER

Staying with the theme of apples, cider is a traditional English alcoholic drink, often associated with the 'West Country' (Cornwall, Somerset, Devon) but also found in more northerly parts such as Worcestershire and Herefordshire.

Real farm-brewed cider bears little resemblance to the bottled variety sold in shops. It is flat, with no fizz, and has a complex flavour which differs from county to county and farm to farm. Aficionados can detect not merely the variety of cider apple used (cider apples are usually small and inedible in their raw state), but also many other notes, such as straw, cow-dung, chicken-dung, cheese, horse-dung, other dung, mud and bees. This is not surprising, given how cider is made. The apples are collected where they lie, covered in whatever animals have left on them, many half-rotten or half-eaten by insects. Unwashed, they are pulped and strained through straw or hessian, then fermented in plastic drums. The final product is sold, often illegally, in half-gallon plastic polypins.

In the past it was considered a good idea to add a dead cockerel to the fermenting liquid, but this practice is either no longer observed or no longer admitted to.

101.

VISIT A BEER FESTIVAL

The English have a problem with alcohol. Politicians, social workers and the medical profession agree: the amount English people drink leads to street violence, liver disease, days lost from work, premature death, child abuse, pimples and marital breakdown. In 2012 the government proposed drastic increases in the price of shop-bought alcohol to prevent drinkers 'preloading' at home before going out to pubs and clubs, but drinkers shrugged and went without food. There's something about being roaring drunk, stripped to the waist and with a barely comprehensible chant of 'It's coming home, it's coming home' emerging from your lips, that is indispensable to English life.

However, there is also 'responsible drinking' in England. It really exists. It's the sort of thing encouraged by CAMRA, the Campaign for Real Ale, founded in 1977 as a reaction against the standardization of pub lager and bitter. CAMRA and its supporters are as concerned with the flavour and provenance of beer as its intoxicating properties: beer, according to this philosophy, is a healthy part of a well-balanced diet. CAMRA sponsors numerous beer festivals up and down the country, annually attended by thousands of people. These festivals feature a vast variety of different cask ales, as well as independently made lagers, ciders, perries, porters, stouts and other drinks. Small 1/3 pint glasses known as 'nips' have recently been introduced to maximize the number of ales that punters can sample without vomiting or losing consciousness. If there is a healthier future to the English drinking culture, this is probably it, but the Chief Medical Officer shouldn't hold his breath.

102.

BOIL VEGETABLES FOR AS LONG AS IT TAKES FOR THEM TO LOSE ANY FLAVOUR, TEXTURE OR COLOUR

In traditional English cooking, the vegetable is an afterthought, an adjunct to the main meat dish. 'Meat and two veg' is the applicable phrase, the type of 'veg' – green beans, potatoes, broccoli, carrots or Brussels sprouts – being interchangeable. They are prepared by boiling for a good half hour, rendering them down until they approach the consistency of soft mud, or, in extreme cases, soup. When the process is complete, the water the vegetables have been boiled in will have more nutritional value than the vegetables themselves.

This is largely a thing of the past. English cuisine has taken a good hard look at itself over the past few years, and vegetables are now served in English homes and restaurants with a little more crunch. But the traditional mud-textured vegetable can still be found if one knows where to look. Day centres for the elderly are good places; retirement homes; institutional care of any kind, particularly for the mentally handicapped. The criterion is that the residents can't talk back or complain, and may only possess gums. Any horrified visitor who has decanted their parents or relatives into such a gastronomic time-warp will be told: 'They like them like that.'

Of course, for large swathes of the English population, the whole question of how long to boil vegetables is a non-starter. Pizza comes with its own vegetables.

Acknowledgements

Thanks to Oli, Clement, James, Isambard, John Swinfield, Tina Potter, Louise Øhrstrøm, Josie Moysey, Jane Moysey, Ole Baxter, Barbara, Alice Risely, Aleksandra Borawska, Snowlion, Rob, Ben, Carrol Dexter and Felicity Ash-Boutall.